Innovation and Impact

The mission of **The Coming of Age of the Education Doctorate** series is to present volumes of research and work focused on the improvement of the Education Doctorate (EdD) and, over the course of the past 14 years, that faculty and schools of education around the US and the world have made to professionalize this degree for the advanced preparation of educational practitioners. Specifically, this series will highlight efforts to improve the purpose, curriculum, and milestone experiences of the degree, in addition to highlighting the work of those who have graduated from redesigned EdD programs. The series will consist of print books, e-books, and fractional digital content for faculty, pre-service teachers, practitioners, and libraries.

Titles in the Series

Challenges in (Re)designing EdD Programs: Supporting Change with Learning Cases edited by Jill A. Perry (2023)

Reclaiming the Education Doctorate: A Guidebook for (re)Designing EdD Programs by Jill A. Perry (2024)

Teaching Critical Inquiry and Applied Research in EdD Programs: Moving Beyond Traditional Methods by Christopher Benedetti and Amanda Covarrubias (2023)

Transforming Identities: How EdD Programs Develop Practitioners into Scholar-Practitioners edited by Stephen J. Pape, Camille L. Bryant, Ranjini Mahinda JohnBull, and Karen S. Karp (2023)

Innovation and Impact: The Origins and Elements of EdD Program Excellence edited by W. Kyle Ingle and Harriette Thurber Rasmussen (2024)

The IMPACT of the Scholarly Practitioner Doctorate: Exercising Socially Just Leadership and Making Equitable Change edited by Stephanie Smith Budhai and Deanna Hill (2024)

The Importance of the Dissertation in Practice (DiP): A Resource Guide for EdD Students, Their Committee Members and Advisors, and Departmental and University Leaders Involved with EdD Programs by Kimberlee Everson, Kelly M. Torres, Lynn Hemmer, Suha Tamim (2024)

The Disquisition: An Equity-Driven Capstone for Leadership Preparation Programs (Working title) by Jess Weiler and Emily Virtue (2024)

Social Justice Praxis in EdD Programs by Ignacio Hernández and Alexia Theresa Pimentel (2024)

Dr. Jill Alexa Perry is the Executive Director of the Carnegie Project on the Educational Doctorate (CPED) and an Associate Professor of Practice in the Educational Foundations, Organizations and Policy at the University of Pittsburgh. Her research focuses on professional doctorate preparation in education, organizational change in higher education, and faculty leadership roles. Currently she is researching the ways EdD programs teach practitioners to utilize research evidence. She teaches and coaches how to teach Improvement Science in EdD programs. Her books include *The Improvement Science Dissertation in Practice*, *The EdD and the Scholarly Practitioner*, and *In Their Own Words: A Journey to the Stewardship of the Practice in Education*. Dr. Perry is a graduate of the University of Maryland, where she received her Ph.D. in International Education Policy. She holds an MA in Higher Education Administration and a BA in Spanish and International Studies from Boston College. She has over 25 years of experience in leadership and program development in education and teaching experience at the elementary, secondary, undergraduate, and graduate levels in the US and abroad. She is a Fulbright Scholar (Germany) and a returned Peace Corps Volunteer (Paraguay).

Innovation and Impact

The Origins and Elements of Ed.D. Program Excellence

EDITED BY W. Kyle Ingle and Harriette Thurber Rasmussen

Myers Education Press

Gorham, Maine

Published by Myers Education Press, LLC
P.O. Box 424
Gorham, ME 04038

Myers Education Press is an academic publisher specializing in books, e-books, and digital content in the field of education. All of our books are subjected to a rigorous peer review process and produced in compliance with the standards of the Council on Library and Information Resources.

Library of Congress Cataloging-in-Publication Data available from Library of Congress.

13-digit ISBN 978-1-9755-0545-5 (paperback)
13-digit ISBN 978-1-9755-0546-2 (library networkable e-edition)
13-digit ISBN 978-1-9755-0547-9 (consumer e-edition)

Printed in the United States of America.

All first editions printed on acid-free paper that meets the American National Standards Institute Z39-48 standard.

Cover design by Teresa Legrange.

DEDICATION

We dedicate this book to faculty members in doctoral programs who give their time, energy, and skills in pursuit of critical reflection and continuous program improvement for the benefit of their university, program, fellow faculty members, students, and alumni.

CONTENTS

ACKNOWLEDGMENTS

There are a number of individuals who were integral to the preparation and publication of this edited book. First, we thank the contributing authors. These individuals serve in crucial leadership roles within their Ed.D. programs, engaging in critical reflection and continuous program improvement with key stakeholders, and generating what inevitably became award-winning Program of the Year applications for their CPED member institutions. Without them, we would not have stories, lessons, and innovative program design features to share with faculty members at institutions currently offering Ed.D. programs or considering the creation of Ed.D. programs. Thanks for your willingness to share your insights and experiences. In so doing, you bring further recognition to your programs and institutions.

We would also like to thank Dr. Jill A. Perry. Dr. Perry wears many hats. She serves as Professor of Practice at the University of Pittsburgh, Executive Director of the Carnegie Project on the Education Doctorate, and Editor of *The Coming of Age of the Education Doctorate Series*, which is published by Myers Education Press. Were it not for her reaching out to us and encouraging us to develop and submit a proposal, this edited book would not have come to fruition.

Lastly, we would like to thank the staff at Myers Education Press for their able guidance and support throughout the publication process. Specifically, we thank Mr. Chris Myers, President and Publisher, and Ms. Stephanie Gabaree, Production Manager. We very much appreciate all the work they both do for authors and editors such as ourselves. Thanks so much for making this process an easy one to navigate.

—W. Kyle Ingle and Harriette Thurber Rasmussen

FOREWORD

JILL A. PERRY, PH.D.
Carnegie Project on the Education Doctorate & University of Pittsburgh

The mission of *The Coming of Age of the Education Doctorate* series is to present volumes of research and work focused on the (re)design of the Education Doctorate (Ed.D.). I created the book series to showcase the past 16+ years of efforts that faculty and schools of education around the United States and the world have undertaken to professionalize this degree for the advanced preparation of educational practitioners. Specifically, this series highlights efforts to enhance and enrich the purpose, curriculum, and milestone experiences in the Ed.D. while spotlighting the work of those who have graduated from (re)designed Ed.D. programs or been involved in the (re)design, delivery, and coordination of their Ed.D. programs.

I chose this volume because it offers the "proofing sites" (Perry & Imig, 2008) the Carnegie Project on the Education Doctorate (CPED) sought through its reclaiming of the Education Doctorate. Allow me to explain. In the beginning of CPED, 25 schools and colleges of education came together to rethink and redesign the Ed.D. to be the strongest professional degree in education. The hope was that in 3 years, we would have exemplars of (re)designed doctoral programs that better prepared educational leaders with the skills, knowledge, and dispositions needed to improve the educational institutions they served. Along the way, however, we discovered that no one-size-fits-all model would work for the Ed.D., given the variety of fields education serves, the variety of institutions of higher education, and the variety of practitioners who seek the degree. To continue the work, we adopted a Framework© that consisted of a new definition of the Ed.D., a set of guiding principles, and a set of design concepts (see http://cped.org) that were flexible enough to allow any type of institution to serve a multitude of practitioners across all fields of education.

Still seeking the idea of proofing sites, we looked to the work of the Sloan Foundation and the Council of Graduate Schools and their work to create the professional sciences masters' recognition process (see Professional Science Master's, n.d., for more details). CPED established a committee of members who researched a variety of processes (from recognition to accreditation) to develop a formal recognition of the CPED-influenced Ed.D. programs that had achieved the CPED Framework. After 4 years of work, the committee put forth a process at the 2014 convening in St. Louis, Missouri. Much to our surprise, the members rejected the recognition process, claiming it felt too constraining and more like accreditation than recognition. Though taken aback, we recognized that our members wanted the freedom to continue to experiment and (re)design programs that best fit their students, faculty, and employers' needs. Being held to a process that required "proving" they had met the CPED Framework© felt constraining.

The work of the recognition committee did not fall by the wayside unused, however. Instead, their efforts shifted to a new process—one that awarded members for self-evaluating and presenting their Ed.D. programs to a committee of peers. The Program of the Year Award was launched in 2017. Through the work of the committee, which is comprised of and led by CPED members, including those who have won the award, the process is designed to offer members the opportunity to evaluate their program against the CPED Framework© and to identify the areas where their program has excelled. The winners of the award have given us a new kind of proofing site, one where faculty and administrators share their efforts to (re)design and continuously improve an Ed.D. that serves practitioners.

The University of Missouri Statewide Ed.D. program was the first recipient of the Program of the Year Award. Since then, eight additional institutions have won the award. Each institution is different, serves a different group of practitioners, and is guided by different institutional regulations. Each Ed.D. program is (re)designed around the expertise of the faculty and the needs of a specific set of practitioners to ensure the program meets its contextual needs. The proof these programs have provided is that the CPED Framework©

is a flexible one that allows each Ed.D. to be governed by and to serve their local context while also preparing scholarly practitioners to improve educational organizations. The co-editors of this book offered each award-winning institution an invitation to discuss their programs, as proofing sites for others to look to as models and exemplars, but not necessarily to replicate in their entirety.

The co-editors of this book are exceptionally suited to present this book, having been the co-leaders and designers of the Program of the Year Award committee and process. Through a collaborative process, the co-editors have guided the chapter authors to write a comprehensive picture of what it means to incorporate the CPED Framework© into an Ed.D. (re)design and how to go about evaluating and presenting that design in order to win the prestigious CPED award.

In the ongoing quest to distinguish the Education Doctorate as the professional practice doctorate in education, this volume is a major contribution because it helps the reader to see how the featured award-winning Ed.D. programs evolved and what it took to create an award-winning Ed.D. program (re)design. To this end, the chapters in this book offer textual representations of the CPED Framework© and push our understanding of what a professional practice doctorate in education can be.

References

Carnegie Project on the Education Doctorate. (n.d.). The Carnegie Project on the Education Doctorate: A knowledge forum on the Ed.D. https://www.cped.org/

Perry, J. A., & Imig, D.G. (2008). A stewardship of practice in education. *Change: The Magazine of Higher Learning, 40*(6), 42–49, DOI: 10.3200/CHNG.40.6.42-49

Professional Science Master's. (n.d.). Professional Science Master's: An innovative graduate degree designed to combine advanced STEM training while simultaneously developing highly valued workplace skills. https://www.professionalsciencemasters.org/

CHAPTER ONE

Framing and Featuring Innovative Ed.D. Programs

W. KYLE INGLE AND
HARRIETTE THURBER RASMUSSEN

In this edited volume, we focus on the Carnegie Project for the Education Doctorate's (CPED) Program of the Year (POY) Award winners, seeking to highlight programs recognized for the distinctive and innovative ways they prepare scholar-practitioners. The award-winners' stories featured in this book will illustrate the mission of CPED, which is to "transform the advanced preparation of educational professionals to lead through scholarly practice for the improvement of individuals and communities" (CPED, n.d.-a), and how the award served as a resource to inform the design of new and existing Ed.D. programs. In so doing, we provide further recognition of the award-winning institutions. Furthermore, this book may serve as a means of diffusing innovations, stimulating change, and advancing social justice within and beyond Ed.D.-awarding institutions.

Regardless of whether the reader is from a CPED or non-CPED member institution, we argue that the key to real impact on institutional goals lies within the process components of these innovations: how the award-winning institutions developed them and the subsequent reflective self-study component of the award process. The award process requires institutional self-awareness and examination of whether and how the intent of the innovation had its desired impact. This book illuminates the essential and ongoing nature of self-study to ensure long-term programmatic viability, quality, and adaptability. Readers will explore internal processes of programmatic transformation, including aspirations or challenges that led to program redesign.

The CPED POY Award winners are selected, in part, by the ways in which their innovations are expected to cause CPED members to grapple with something new and different. This book intends for its readers to do the same as they read about innovation in areas such as equitable advising, social justice–driven research, and practitioner impacts. To be clear, this book features award-winning programs, but we want it to be more than *show-and-tell.* The heart of this book is the process stories of these award-winning institutions as they sought to further institutional and programmatic goals through innovation and impact.

In this introductory chapter, we delve into the existing research on the role that recognitions and awards play in organizations and institutions. We then turn our attention to CPED and its POY Award. We provide a brief history of the consortium and an overview of the award, including its stated purpose, submission requirements, committee structure, activities, and rubrics. We also illustrate how CPED involves faculty from member institutions in determining what to emphasize in the award (e.g., innovations and outcomes). Importantly, in this first chapter, we establish the framing and guidance provided to the chapter authors, discussing Rogers' (2003) diffusion of innovations theory so that readers will draw upon transferable elements, considered contextually as related to their own institutions. We also provide key technical terms (e.g., proofing sites, innovation) to ensure that the reader has sufficient understanding of relevant terms.

Awards and Recognitions: A Brief Review of the Literature

A wide range of organizations in private, public, and nonprofit sectors establish awards to recognize the accomplishments of individuals, teams, programs, or other organizations. These vary in their notoriety, ranging from the internationally renowned Nobel Prize (Zuckerman, 1977) to those that are more obscure and local in nature, such as a school or district recognizing its Teacher of the Year. Among fields, Frey (2006) characterizes academia as having an elaborate and extensive system of awards. Researchers suggest that prestigious awards in academia are associated with strong positive effects on the recipients' subsequent performance, especially in high-quality research publications and citations (Chan et al., 2014).

Awards and recognitions are both pecuniary and nonpecuniary (Frey, 2006). The aforementioned Nobel Prize is an example of the former. Winners, selected annually, receive a cash prize as part of the honor. Another pecuniary award category is what scholars refer to as inducement prizes (Khan, 2015; Williams, 2012). With inducement prizes, recipients receive remuneration and recognition as a reward for developing an innovation or solution to a persistent difficult problem. Khan (2015) highlights one of the most well-known inducement prizes. In 1714, the British Parliament created a governmental body—the Commissioners for the Discovery of the Longitude at Sea, also known as the Longitude Board—and a reward for any individual(s) able to gauge longitude accurately at sea. Khan and others (e.g., Landes, 1983; Sobel, 1996) note the difficulties that John Harrison, the individual credited with solving the challenges associated with gauging longitude at sea, encountered along the way. He struggled for years to come up with a solution and receive remuneration for his hard work. Khan states that, "a full forty-seven years elapsed before Harrison actually received compensation, and it was from another source than the Longitude Board" (2015, p. 635).

Frey and Gallus (2015) note that while the inclusion of money aids in establishing the seriousness of the award, winners are likely to accept prestigious awards regardless of whether a monetary award accompanies the honor or not. Frey and Gallus also contend that prestige and monetary awards are not necessarily commensurate. They note that the recipients of the Nobel Peace Prize, an annual award that has wide-ranging international notoriety, receive a cash prize that is approximately 46% the amount of Switzerland's Balzan Prize for Humanity, Peace and Fraternity among Peoples. In spite of having a larger cash award and being bestowed every 3 to 5 years, the Balzan Prize arguably enjoys far less prestige or notoriety than the Nobel Prize (2015, pp. 82–83). Frey and Gallus highlight that creating and giving awards without a cash prize is relatively cheap for the awarding body compared to those that do. However, the award still holds value for recipients by recognizing their talents, skills, and commitment. As an example, consider the University Council for Educational Administration's (UCEA) Jack A. Culbertson Award, which is "presented annually to an outstanding junior professor of educational administration in recognition of their contributions to the field" (UCEA, n.d., para 4). Receiving this award externally from a professional association may reinforce the pre-tenure candidate's case for tenure and promotion. This honor may also signal quality for other institutions seeking to recruit high-quality, high-profile candidates for a faculty search or lead to grants and contracts. Scholars have observed this phenomenon among Oscar recipients, who subsequently realize an increase in employment opportunities and income (Nelson et al., 2001).

The awarding organizations, institutions, and associations send signals both internally and externally as to what they value through the honors they create, potentially yielding positive public relations and exposure (Frey & Gallus, 2015). Researchers also note the special relationship that may develop between the award giver and recipient, such as greater loyalty to the awarding organization in the form of a greater likelihood of financial support to the award-giving institution (Frey, 2006; Rousseau & Parks, 1993). A recipient of an alumnus/alumna of the year award may donate or increase the amount of donations to the awarding university—even though such donations are not a contractual obligation. They may do so out of a sense of loyalty to their alma mater and an appreciation of the honor bestowed upon them. In the case of program awards such as CPED's POY Award, winning does not yield direct benefits to the individuals who developed and submitted the award application, but it may yield indirect benefits to the program as evidenced by increases in interest, applications, and admissions into the program.

Eligibility requirements, nomination procedures, and selection processes for awards vary widely. In the field of education, professional associations such as the American Education Research Association (AERA) establish guidelines for its members on the creation of awards, limits on the number of awards, selection processes, and timelines for decision-making and presentations. Specifying the requisite qualifications, nomination processes, and the number of recipients seeks to establish the legitimacy and prestige of the award. Having too many recipients of an award may adversely affect public perceptions of the award and the prestige of receiving it (e.g., Loveless & DiPerna, 2006). As Frey (2006) documents, "awards are in demand only if perceived as valuable to recipients because they signal distinction to other persons. If an award is easy to get, it loses this value and no longer serves this purpose" (p. 381).

As one can see, awards and recognitions vary in their characteristics and components. These include:

- Who established the award?
- When did the individual or organization establish the award?
- Why did the individual or organization establish the award?
- What is the process by which the candidates and recipients are nominated, selected, and notified (e.g., self-nominations, peer-nominations)?
- How many recipients are there to be?
- When, where, and who presents the award?
- What does the recipient receive (e.g., cash prize, certificate, ribbon, plaque)?
- How do the recipient's peers and the public perceive the award?

These components become relevant as we turn our attention to a specific educational association (CPED) and its program of the year award—the focus of this edited volume.

A Brief History of CPED and its Program of the Year Award

The Doctor of Education (Ed.D.) traces its origins back to 1921 when the faculty of Harvard's Graduate School of Education created the degree program (Perry, 2014). The faculty at Harvard saw the Ed.D. as a means of providing advanced graduate education for experienced teachers seeking advancement within their schools and districts (Cremin, 1978). Since then, Ed.D. programs have proliferated across institutions of higher learning in the United States and abroad, not to mention the development and proliferation of additional professional practice doctorates (PPD) degrees, such as the Doctor of Business Administration, Doctor of Information Technology, and Doctor of Project Management (Buss et al., 2017). Despite its Ivy League roots, scholars have been critical of Ed.D. programs and educational leadership programs generally, regardless of their level or classification, e.g., Master's, Specialist's, or Doctor of Education (Elmore, 2000; Hess & Kelly, 2005). Critics questioned what, if any, distinctions existed between the Ed.D. and Ph.D.—and have even called for the dissolution of Ed.D. programs (e.g., Clifford & Guthrie, 1990; Deering, 1998; Levine, 2005, 2007). Concerns ranged from the content and appropriateness of the programs' curricula, the lack of clinical experiences, the balance of theory and practice, and the research they produced, particularly regarding Ed.D. programs (Levine, 2005, 2007).

Founded in 2007 with support from the Carnegie Foundation for the Advancement of Teaching and the Council for Academic Deans of Research Education Institutions (CADREI), CPED emerged as a response to Dr. Lee Shulman and colleagues' (2006) call for schools of education to define and differentiate the Ed.D. from the Ph.D. or "risk becoming increasingly impotent in carrying out their primary missions—the advancement of knowledge and the preparation of quality practitioners" (p. 25). Shulman eventually became CPED's first president, working with faculty members from 25 founding member institutions to establish a set of principles, architecture, and models for programmatic and institutional change (Perry & Imig, 2008). In September 2010, CPED won a $700,000 grant from the Fund for the Improvement of Post-Secondary Education (FIPSE). In 2017, CPED garnered additional financial support from the William T. Grant Foundation, providing the consortium with $500,000 to examine research evidence used by graduates from four CPED member institutions (Firestone et al., 2021).

Since 2007, the consortium has expanded its membership to over 130 universities that have committed financial and human resources to work together in a critical examination of the Ed.D. through dialog, experimentation, critical feedback, and evaluation. Headquartered at the University of Pittsburgh, CPED now hosts annual convenings, sponsors a peer-reviewed journal, and continues to expand its membership and activities. In 2013, the consortium established its Dissertation in Practice (DiP) Award. In 2017, CPED established the David G. Imig Distinguished Service Award to recognize individuals and their contributions to CPED's vision and mission.

Following its original intent to develop "proofing sites" that exemplify how the association and its members might better prepare future stewards of practice (Imig et al., 2009), CPED established the POY Award in 2017. The award honors "one or more institutions whose CPED-influenced programs show themselves to be distinctive, innovative, and useful to other CPED members" (CPED, n.d.-b). In bestowing the POY Award, CPED seeks to not only recognize programs for their distinctive, innovative, and impactful designs and characteristics, it seeks to involve the award-winning programs' faculty, staff, and students as active contributors to the consortium's knowledge base. CPED recognizes the award-winning programs publicly at its annual convenings, providing a means by which other CPED member institutions may learn about the programs' innovative features through presentations given at the award ceremony, invited learning exchanges at CPED's annual convenings, and online resources that highlight the award-winning programs. CPED also encourages faculty from the award-winning programs to submit manuscripts to its peer-reviewed academic journal, *Impacting Education: The Journal for Transforming Professional Practice* (IE). The award-winning institution receives an engraved crystal trophy and receives special acknowledgment at CPED's website. While POY Award winners receive no cash prize, the award provides a valuable point of pride for the award-winning institution, the program, its faculty, staff, students, and alumni—and serves as a strong recruitment tool for the Ed.D. program.

A committee representing approximately 10% of institutional members guides the Program of the Year Award process. While not a prerequisite of membership, faculty members from previously selected award-winning institutions receive invitations to serve on the committee after receiving the award. The committee includes two members who serve as co-chairs, organizing and facilitating the work and liaising between the committee and CPED's headquarters. Their work includes proposing a timeline for the award each year, scheduling meetings with the full committee to establish the annual call for applications, review procedures, and review scoring rubrics. Each year, this committee determines a focal point for the award (e.g., innovative characteristics of their program, transformational changes to the program, how the program seeks to advance social justice) and quality indicators that guide its selection process. The quality indicators culminate in rubrics used for both a preliminary and a full application, both of which are available to the membership on the CPED website.

Applicants self-nominate for CPED's POY Award. The application process has two phases. The first consists of a preliminary application explaining the program and the ways in which its transformative elements meet institutional and CPED alignment. Doing so are prerequisites for an invitation to submit a full application. This phase is not competitive; the POY Committee determines whether the submitting institution meets the minimal threshold of alignment. Phase two begins when the awards committee invites institutions that meet the threshold to submit a full application, focused only on the focal point for the award (e.g., innovative characteristics of their program, transformational changes to the program, how the program seeks to advance social justice) and its impact on the institution, its faculty, its students, and its community. This final phase is competitive with a rigorous review by the committee members and deep discussions around evidence justifying each member's ratings.

Since its creation in 2017, eight member institutions have received the CPED POY Award (See Table 1.1). Award-winning institutions include both public and private member institutions from across the United States. A majority of the award-winning institutions hold "R1" Carnegie Classifications (doctoral-granting universities with very high research activity). To date, no member institutions from outside of the United States have won the CPED POY Award.

Table 1.1. CPED Program of the Year Award Winners (2017–2022)

Year	Institution	CPED Membership	Institutional Type	Carnegie Classification
2017	University of Missouri	2007	Public	R1
2018	Arizona State University	2007	Public	R1
	University of Hawai'i at Mānoa	2010	Public	R1
2019	Drexel University	2015	Private	R1
2020	University of Florida	2007	Public	R1
2021	Western Carolina University	2014	Public	D/PU

Year	Institution	CPED Membership	Institutional Type	Carnegie Classification
2022	Baylor University	2010	Private	R1
	Northeastern University	2014	Private	R1

Note: R1, doctoral universities – very high research activity; D/PU, doctoral/professional universities.

Innovation Diffusion Theory: A Primer

The theoretical framing for this volume and the chapters herein is diffusion of innovations theory. Popularized by communication theorist Everett Rogers (1962, 2003), his theory began as a doctoral study of how agricultural innovations spread across rural communities. Rogers would go on to publish his seminal work, *Diffusion of Innovations*, in 1962. Since then, diffusion of innovations theory has informed the work of scholars in agriculture (e.g., Abdulai & Huffman, 2005) and communications (e.g., Srivastava & Moreland, 2012). It would also find applications in other fields, such as business (Brouthers et al., 2016), health care (e.g., Berwick, 2003), information technology (e.g., Jeyaraj et al., 2006), public administration (e.g., Zhu & Zhang, 2016), and education (e.g., Cohen-Vogel et al., 2008). Now in its fifth edition, Rogers' *Diffusion of Innovations* (2003) continues to remain relevant in research. The variation among innovation diffusion studies across these various research fields relates to the type of innovation around which the research is focused and the units of analysis across which the innovations diffuse (Nice, 1994). For example, sociologists often focus on the diffusion of innovations among individuals (e.g., Copp et al., 1958). In public health and medicine, researchers examining the diffusion of drugs, medical equipment, or practices focus on diffusion between healthcare professionals and institutions (e.g., Berwick, 2003). In the fields of political science and policy studies, the primary units of analysis are governments—local, state, and national (e.g., Mintrom & Vergari, 1998).

Innovation diffusion is the process by which an innovation spreads among the members of a social system, in this case the internal and external communities of Ed.D.-granting institutions.

Rogers (2003) identifies four main elements that influence the spread of an innovation (see Table 1.2). The first is the innovation itself, defined as "an idea, practice, or object that is perceived as new by an individual or other unit of adoption" (p. 12). The characteristics and perceptions of an innovation explain different rates of adoption (see Table 1.3). The second is communications channels, which are the "means by which messages get from one individual to another" (Rogers, 2003, p. 18). The third is the element of time, representing how long it takes between first learning about an innovation to adopting it. It also refers to the relative earliness/lateness by which individuals or other units of analysis (e.g., organizations) adopt an innovation and how fast these units of analysis adopt an innovation in a given period. The fourth and final element is the social system, which refers to the interrelated units engaged in solving problems and pursuing common goals.

Researchers have documented the role that professional organizations and associations play in the diffusion of innovations. For example, Cohen-Vogel et al. (2008) revealed professional associations, including the National Governors' Association (NGA), the Southern Governors' Association (SGA), the Southern Regional Education Board (SREB), and the National Association of State Student Grants and Aids Programs (NASSGAP), as integral to the diffusion of broad-based merit aid programs in the southeastern United States. The NGA, SGA, and SREB provided venues for policymakers and their aides to discuss shared problems and possible policy solutions (e.g., broad-based merit aid programs). Other organizations, like NASSGAP, served as a networking opportunity for state scholarship administrators to make connections with colleagues in other states with whom they would discuss programmatic details once their states enacted merit aid. Others (e.g., Deephouse & Heugens, 2009; Scheiber, 2015) have shown how business/news media, trade journals, and/or professional associations serve as sources of information and means of diffusing policies on corporate social responsibility and codes of conduct within business and industry.

As a consortium of institutions of higher learning committed to the critical examination of Ed.D. programs, CPED is such a social system. CPED and faculty from its member institutions collaborated in the development of a framework for Ed.D. program design/redesign "that supports creating quality, rigorous practitioner preparation while honoring the local context of each member institution" (n.d.-a, para. 5). Indeed, the POY requires that a self-nominating institution provide evidence of how their Ed.D. program aligns with CPED principles and design concepts as a condition for an invitation to submit a full application. CPED's convenings, journal, reports, and websites all serve as means of reinforcing its framework for Ed.D. program design/redesign and for potentially diffusing innovative elements.

Table 1.2. Elements of Rogers' Diffusion of Innovation Model

Element	Definition	Example(s)
Innovation	An idea that is "perceived as new by an individual or other unit of adoption" (Rogers, 2003, p. 12).	A CPED-member institution develops and validates an instrument used to measure scholar-practitioner growth in leadership for equity.
Communication Channels	These are the "means by which messages get from one individual to another" (Rogers, 2003, p. 18).	A CPED-member institution shares the instrument by means of research presentations at professional conferences (e.g., UCEA, AERA, CPED). The CPED-member institution wins the Program of the Year Award, in part on the strength and utility of its instrument that was developed. The award-winning institution is asked to discuss the innovation at a special session of CPED and at the awards reception.
Time	This refers to the amount of time it takes by which (1) "an individual passes from first knowledge of an innovation through its adoption or rejection"; (2) "the relative earliness/lateness with which an innovation is adopted"; and (3) "an innovation's rate of adoption in a system, usually measured as the number of members of the system who adopt the innovation in a given period of time" (Rogers, 2003, p. 20).	1. An institutional representative attends an annual convening of CPED and learns about the instrument. This individual shares the information with their colleagues, who want to learn more. They reach out to the innovative CPED program that developed the instrument and ask permission to review the instrument. The institution shares it and the questing institution adopts it the next academic year, becoming an early adopter of the innovation. 2. Six CPED-member institutions adopt the innovation, becoming early adopters of the innovation 3. A majority of CPED-member institutions eventually adopt the instrument within 10 years.

Element	Definition	Example(s)
Social System	This refers to the "interrelated units that are engaged in joint problem-solving to accomplish a common goal" (Rogers, 2003, p. 23).	Individual faculty members and other stakeholders within a CPED-influenced doctoral program at a state university. It may also refer to an association of doctoral granting institutions (e.g., CPED), which have committed resources to work together to undertake a critical examination of the doctorate in education (Ed.D.) through dialog, experimentation, critical feedback and evaluation.

We asked the contributing authors to integrate terms and concept of diffusion of innovation theory into their discussions by considering:

- The motivations for the innovative elements and design features highlighted in their application;
- Where they sought ideas to develop innovative elements and design features for their Ed.D.;
- Ways in which they borrowed and adapted an innovation from elsewhere, thus becoming an agent of diffusion themselves;
- The communication channels to develop or adapt the innovative features of their award-winning program;
- Contacts with other institutions since winning the CPED POY Award to learn more about their program and its design features;
- The social systems engaged in developing their innovative program features;
- Engagement in social systems after winning the award that may have contributed to further adaptation.

Rogers (2003) explains the innovation process in an organization as two broad activities. The first is *initiation*, consisting of information gathering, conceptualization, and planning, leading to the decision to adopt. The second is *implementation*, consisting of the events, actions, and decisions involved in putting the innovation into use (see Figure 1.1). The decision to adopt, shown as a dotted line, divides two stages of initiation from three stages of implementation (p. 421).

Broad Activities	Stage	Description
Initiation	1. Agenda-setting	The stage in which an organizational problem (or problems) may create a perceived need for innovation.
	2. Matching	The stage in which there is the fitting of a problem from the organization's agenda with an innovation.
Implementation	3. Redefining/Restructuring	The stage in which the innovation is modified and re-invented to fit the organization and organizational structures are altered.
	4. Clarifying	The stage in which the relationship between the organization and the innovation is defined more clearly.
	5. Routinizing	The stage in which the innovation becomes an ongoing element in the organization's activities and loses its identity.

Figure 1.1. Five Stages in the Innovation Process in Organizations

We asked the contributing authors to integrate these terms into their discussions by posing explicit questions for them to address in their chapters. For example:

- When did they and their program faculty become aware of problems needing redress in their Ed.D. program?
- How did they explore potential options/solutions to address the problem(s) needing innovation and improvement?
- How did they and their program faculty redefine/restructure an existing practice to fit your doctoral program and its needs?
- How did they seek input from stakeholders (e.g., students, alumni, college curriculum committees) in structuring their proposed innovative Ed.D. features to ensure its acceptance, approval, and clarity?
- How did they ingrain their adopted innovative features in practice?
- Have they revisited their initial innovative design features since their initial adoption and have these been adapted further?

Characterizing Innovation

Rogers identifies five characteristics of innovation: relative advantage, compatibility, adaptability, trialability, and observability (see Table 1.3). These aspects of innovation serve as organizing principles for the discursive sections that reflect upon the processes that drove the program to innovate their program, seeking a range of alternatives and how to assess their fit for their own Ed.D. programs, its goals, and those of the institution.

Table 1.3. Rogers' Five Characteristics of an Innovation

Characteristic	Definition	Example (Weight Loss)
Relative Advantage	The degree to which a particular innovation is perceived to be the best among other alternatives. Individuals and organizations identify a number of potential innovations that all seek to accomplish a desired end.	Diet Exercise Medication Surgery
Trialability	The degree in which an innovation can be experienced firsthand on a limited basis.	A regimen of diet and exercise is more trialable than surgery.
Observability	The degree to which an innovation and its outcomes can be seen by others likely to adopt it.	Weight loss medication is less likely to be adopted if its potential adopters are unaware of its existence and results.
Compatibility	The degree to which an innovation is seen as consistent with existing values, previous experiences, and needs of the potential adopter.	An individual with prior bad experiences or limited success with weight loss medications may be less likely to adopt another based on those prior experiences. If an individual perceives the claims of weight loss medication advertising to be "too good to be true," then the individual may be less likely to adopt such a product.
Complexity	The degree to which an innovation is perceived as difficult to understand or utilize.	Independent research may suggest that diet and exercise is more effective than weight loss medications, but the regimen of diet and exercise may be perceived as too time-consuming or difficult.

We offered these as guidance to the contributing authors, providing an example (weight loss) for illustration purposes. Again, we provided questions for our authors to address in their submissions. Specifically:

- What alternatives did they consider when seeking to address perceived problems or design features needing innovation?
- Why did they select the alternative(s) that featured innovative design features in their award-winning Ed.D. program?
- To what extent were the selected alternatives visible, available, and "trialable" for them?
- Assuming that the selected alternatives were trialable, to what extent did they try them out beforehand? How did they do this?
- Did they explore possible innovations by observing other institutions or researching what they were doing along these lines?
- How did they assess the compatibility of proposed innovative features with key institutional stakeholders?
- Were some potential innovations too complex or a poor fit for the context of their Ed.D. program? If so, how did they know?

We also asked about decision-making processes. Rogers (2003) delineates a five-stage decision-making model (see Table 1.4).

Table 1.4. Rogers' Innovation Decision-Making Process

Stage	Description
1. Knowledge	In this stage, the individual or organization is first exposed to an innovation, but lacks information about it.
2. Persuasion	In this stage, the individual or organization is interested in the innovation and actively seeks out more information about the innovation.
3. Decision	In this stage, the individual or organization examines whatever information that has been collected on the innovation, weighs its various advantages and disadvantages, and decides whether to adopt or reject the innovation.
4. Implementation	In this stage, the individual or organization employs the innovation, informing decision-making on its utility.
5. Confirmation	In this stage, the individual or organization finalizes decision-making as to whether to continue using the innovation or not.

We asked the contributing authors to integrate these terms into their discussions by posing further questions:

- What characteristics of their institution and program led them to seek information on possible innovations to address perceived problems or design features needing innovation?
- Where did they seek knowledge and information to address perceived problems or design features needing innovation?
- How difficult was persuading stakeholders within their Ed.D. program (e.g., students, faculty, curriculum committees, etc.) to build interest in the innovative program features highlighted in their award-winning application?
- To what extent did the perceived characteristics of the innovation (e.g., relative advantage, compatibility, complexity, trialability, observability) play a role in their efforts to persuade key stakeholders within their institution?
- How onerous was the decision-making process regarding whether to adopt or reject the innovation?
- How has the implementation of their innovative program feature(s) adapted since its implementation and since winning the award?

Within this framing, we asked the invited chapter authors to tell the story of their award in ways that encourage continued reflection about the process, including how writing about it at this stage provided new insight and direction.

Overall Structure of the Chapters

The contributing authors for this volume are faculty member(s) involved in developing their award-winning institution's application. Diffusion of innovation concepts guided the authors in constructing their chapters, which consisted of dual components: (1) innovative programs that drive social justice and (2) how they and their institution developed and sustained their innovative programs. The latter component will shed light on three self-study processes related to these award-winning programs:

1) The process of creating the featured innovative program;
2) The process of applying for the program of the year award; and
3) The process of writing the journey and considering the impact of the program of the year award on their institution, including any reinvention/adaptations.

Taken together, readers will have a window into the processes by which program faculty adapted and innovated their programs, how and where they looked for solutions, how the innovative programs took shape, and the impacts of the program on various outcomes. While these chapters are relatively consistent in their format, descriptive, thick explanations, we emphasized our desire for stories that (we hope) are interesting, informative, and transferable to other institutions of higher learning. Each chapter concludes with a coda written *after* the initial chapter was constructed and through a guided reflective process with one of the editors. Our intent was to provoke deeper reflection and more transferable learning to the reader.

Our concluding chapter serves as a synthesis, reflection, and commentary on the CPED POY award, including lessons learned and reflection on the benefits for its recipients. Importantly, when launching this volume, we could not claim to know these benefits; in fact, we anticipated some surprises. These were uncovered through the process of institutional reflection, followed by our own. Ultimately, the goal of this final chapter is to illuminate aspects of the self-study process that offer potential replication for both Ed.D.-awarding institutions and organizations such as CPED that serve its member institutions in ways that add value to their institutional goals. It brings diffusion of innovation theory into focus, drawing upon each of the chapters to pull themes and collective learning from these award-winning programs, including the self-study and diffusion processes that brought them to fruition. We also highlight the most promising practices, including study templates, discussion questions, or other noted processes, across award winners that most influenced the CPED POY Award Committee in their decision-making. In so doing, we hope to inform the work of faculty within existing Ed.D. programs or those considering the establishment of an Ed.D. program.

References

Abdulai, A., & Huffman, W. E. (2005). The diffusion of new agricultural technologies: The case of crossbred-cow technology in Tanzania. *American Journal of Agricultural Economic, 87*(3), 537–821. https://doi.org/10.1111/j.1467-8276.2005.00753.x

Berwick, D. M. (2003). Disseminating innovations in health care. *Journal of the American Medical Association, 289*(15), 1969–1975. doi:10.1001/jama.289.15.1969

Brouthers, K. D., Geisser, K. D., & Rothlauf, F. Explaining the internationalization of ibusiness firms. *Journal of International Business Studies, 47*(5), 513–534. https://doi.org/10.1057/jibs.2015.20

Buss, R., Zambo, R., Zambo, D., Perry, J. A., & Williams, T. (2017). Faculty members' responses to implementing re-envisioned Ed.D. programs. *Studies in Higher Education, 42*(9), 1624–1640. https://doi.org/10.1080/03075079.2015.1113951

Carnegie Project on the Education Doctorate (CPED). (n.d.-a). Our vision and mission. Retrieved February 8, 2023 from https://www.cpedinitiative.org/vision-mission

Carnegie Project on the Education Doctorate (CPED). (n.d.-b). CPED awards. Retrieved February 8, 2023 from https://www.cpedinitiative.org/awards

Chan, H. F., Frey, B. S., Gallus, J., & Torgler, B. (2014). Academic honors and performance. *Labour Economics, 31*, 188–204. https://doi.org/10.1016/j.labeco.2014.05.005

Clifford, G. J., & J. W. Guthrie. (1988). *Ed school: A brief for a professional education.* University of Chicago Press.

Cohen-Vogel, L., Ingle, W. K., Levine, A. A., & Spence, M. (2008). The "spread" of merit-based college aid: Politics, policy consortia, and interstate competition. *Educational Policy, 22*(3), 339–362. https://doi.org/10.1177/0895904807307059

Copp, J. H., Sill, M. L., & Brown, E. J. (1958). The function of information sources in the farm practice adoption process. *Rural Sociology, 23*, 146–157.

Cremin, L. (1978). *The education of the educating professions.* American Association of Colleges for Teacher Education.

Deephouse, D. L., & Heugens, P. P. (2009). Linking social issues to organizational impact: The role of infomediaries and the infomediary process. *Journal of Business Ethics, 86*, 541–553. https://doi.org/10.1007/s10551-008-9864-3

Deering, T. E. (1998). Eliminating the Doctor of Education degree: It's the right thing to do. *Educational Forum 62*(3), 243–248. https://doi.org/10.1080/00131729808984350

Elmore, R. F. (2000). *Building a new structure for school leadership.* The Albert Shanker Institute.

Firestone, W. A., Perry, J. A., Leland, A. S, & McKeon, R. T. (2021). Teaching research and data use in the education doctorate. *Journal of Research on Leadership Education, 16*(1) 81–102. https://doi.org/10.1177/1942775119872231

Frey, B. S. (2006). Giving and receiving awards. *Perspectives on Psychological Science, 1*(4), 377–388. https://doi.org/10.1111/j.1745-6916.2006.00022.x

Frey, B. S., & Gallus, J. (2015). Awards as non-monetary incentives. *Evidence-based HRM: a Global Forum for Empirical Scholarship, 4*(1), 81–91. https://doi.org/10.1108/EBHRM-05-2015-0016

Gallus, J. & Frey, B. S. (2016). Awards: a strategic management perspective. *Strategic Management Journal, 37*(8), 1699–1714. https://doi.org/10.1002/smj.2415

Heinich, N. (2009). The sociology of vocational prizes: Recognition as esteem. *Theory, Culture and Society, 26*(5), 85–107. https://doi.org/10.1177/0263276409106352

Hess, F. M., & Kelly, A. P. (2005). An innovative look, a recalcitrant reality: The politics of principal preparation reform. *Educational Policy, 19*(1), 155–180. https://doi.org/10.1177/0895904804270776

Imig, D., Perry, J. A., & Syed, S. (2009). *Creating rubrics for the assessment of the Ed.D.: Narrative report to the Spencer Foundation.* Carnegie Project on the Education Doctorate.

Jeyaraj, A., Rottman, J. W. & Lacity, M. C. (2006). A review of the predictors, linkages, and biases in IT innovation adoption research. *Journal of Information Technology, 21*(1), 1–23. https://doi.org/10.1057/palgrave.jit.2000056

Khan, B. Z. (2015). Inventing prizes: A historical perspective on innovation awards and technology policy. *Business History Review, 89*(4), 631–660. https://doi.org/10.1017/S0007680515001014

Landes, D. S. (1983). *Revolution in time.* Harvard University Press.

Levine, A. (2005). *Educating school leaders.* The Education Schools Project.

Levine, A. (2007). *Educating researchers.* The Education Schools Project.

Loveless, T., & DiPerna, P. (2006). In praise of mediocrity: Tattered blue ribbons at the Department of Education. *Education Next News, 1*(2). https://www.educationnext.org/in-praise-of-mediocrity/

Mann, K. B. (1988). Recognition programs for academic success: improvement or achievement? *NASSP Bulletin, 72*, 101–102. https://doi.org/10.1177/019263658807251219

Mintrom, M., & Vergari, S. (1998). Policy networks and innovation diffusion: The case of state education reforms. *Journal of Politics, 60*(1), 126–148. https://doi.org/10.2307/2648004

Nelson, R. A., Donihue, M. R., Waldman, D., & Wheaton, C. (2001). What's an Oscar worth? *Economic Inquiry, 39*(1), 1–16. https://doi.org/10.1111/j.1465-7295.2001.tb00046.x

Nice, D. C. (1994). *Policy innovation in state government.* Iowa State University Press.

Perry, J. A. (2014). Changing schools of education through grassroots faculty-led change. *Innovative Higher Education, 39*(2), 155–168. https://doi.org/10.1007/s10755-013-9267-y

Perry, J. A., & Imig, D. G. (2008). A stewardship of practice in education. *Change, 40*(6), 42–48. https://www.jstor.org/stable/40178299

Reschke, B. P., Azoulay, P., & Stuart, T. E. (2018). Status spillovers: The effect of status-conferring prizes on the allocation of attention. *Administrative Science Quarterly, 63*(4), 819–847. DOI: 10.1177/0001839217731997

Rogers, E. M. (1962). *Diffusions of innovations*. The Free Press.

Rogers, E. M. (2003). *Diffusions of innovations* (5th ed.). The Free Press.

Rousseau, D. M., & Parks, J. M. (1993). The contracts of individuals and organizations. *Research in Organizational Behavior, 15*, 1–43.

Scheiber, F. (2015). Dressing up for diffusion: Codes of conduct in the German textile and apparel industry, 1997–2010. *Journal of Business Ethics, 126*, 559–580. https://doi.org/10.1007/s10551-013-1964-z

Shulman, L. S., Golde, C. M., Bueschel, A. C., & Garabedian, K. J. (2006). Reclaiming education's doctorates: A critique and a proposal. *Educational Researcher, 35*(3), 25–32. https://doi.org/10.3102/0013189X035003025

Sobel, D. (1996). *Longitude: The true story of a lone genius who solved the greatest scientific problem of his time*. Penguin Publishing.

Srivastava, J., & Moreland, J. J. (2012) Diffusion of innovations: Communication evolution and influences. *Communication Review, 15*(4), 294–312. http://dx.doi.org/10.1080/10714421.2012.728420

University Council for Educational Administration. (n.d.) About UCEA Awards. Retrieved February 8, 2023 from http://www.ucea.org/opportunities/about-awards/

Williams, H. (2012). Innovation inducement prizes: Connecting research to policy. *Journal of Policy Analysis and Management, 31*(3), 752–776. https://doi.org/10.1002/pam.21638

Zhu, X., & Zhang, Y. (2016). Political mobility and dynamic diffusion of innovation: The spread of municipal pro-business administrative reform in China. *Journal of Public Administration Research and Theory, 26*(3), 535–551. https://doi.org/10.1093/jopart/muv025

Zuckerman, H. (1977). Scientific elite: *Nobel Laureates in the United States*. Free Press.

CHAPTER TWO

The Ed.D. Program and Cycles of Innovation at the University of Missouri

JENNIFER FELLABAUM-TOSTON, CASANDRA HARPER, AND BRADLEY R. CURS

The University of Missouri's (MU) Statewide Cooperative Ed.D. program was created in the mid-1990s to respond to the needs of educational leaders across Missouri. Utilizing a unique cooperative model, five distinct institutions of higher learning in Missouri came together to develop and deliver this Ed.D. program: Missouri State University, Northwest Missouri State University, Southeast Missouri State University, University of Central Missouri, and the University of Missouri. Cohorts consisted of approximately 90 students admitted every 2 years, with an average of 18 students assigned per partner institution. The Statewide Cooperative Ed.D. Program included 2 years of coursework, with 2 summers of up to 12 days of intensive, in-person instruction on the MU campus in Columbia. During the fall and spring semesters, each partner institution delivered coursework at their campuses around the state.

The MU Statewide Cooperative Ed.D. Program (then and now) incorporates four main critical lenses (i.e., content areas) into the curriculum: leadership theory and practice, organizational analysis, educational policy, and content and context of learning. In addition, students engage in research, inquiry, and evaluation coursework to develop the tools necessary to transfer knowledge into practice. Change, ethics, and social justice are threads found throughout the program. Since 1997 when the first cooperative cohort began, over 750 educational leaders have received their Ed.D. degrees through the MU Statewide Cooperative Ed.D. Program.

Our PK-20+ cohort model[1] facilitated collaboration and the sharing of perspectives amongst students and faculty. Representatives from each of the five partner institutions served as the doctoral program's Coordinating Committee, the body responsible for providing input and leadership of the Ed.D. Program. Instructional teams worked together each semester to ensure the integration of content themes across the coursework and that assignments were problem-based, reflective, and aligned with the programmatic learning objectives, providing students with opportunities to apply knowledge and skills from their courses in their laboratories of practice. Upon completion of coursework, students worked on written and oral comprehensive examinations during their third year in the program. Finally, the culminating event was the completion of a dissertation-in-practice that addresses real-world problems within students' own laboratories of practice.

This chapter explores a major cycle of innovation that contributed to our decision to apply for the Carnegie Project on the Education Doctorate's (CPED) inaugural Program of the Year (POY) award. As relevant, we utilize Rogers' (2003) five stages in the innovation process (agenda-setting, matching, redefining/restructuring, clarifying, and routinizing) as a framework for our discussion. This cycle of our redesign effort began with a focus on moving from a traditional five-chapter model often used in Ph.D. programs to a dissertation-in-practice model designed with scholarly practitioners in mind. We then turned to comprehensive exams, followed by "the most extensive curricular redesign since 2000-2001"[2] (MacGregor & Fellabaum, 2016, p. 60), seeking to ensure both scaffolding of the dissertation-in-practice as well as explicit integration of CPED design concepts and principles. Our efforts resulted in adjustments to the vision, mission, programmatic learning outcomes, admissions process, curriculum, comprehensive exams, and dissertation-in-practice. The decision to apply for the POY award in 2017 was in recognition of these efforts and the positive outcomes observed as we implemented these changes. We then describe a second cycle in the coda that began in 2019–2020, following difficult decisions made in response to drastic shifts in the financial stability of the MU Statewide Cooperative Ed.D. Program.

Cycle of Innovation: 2011 to 2015

In 2011, we began efforts to identify ways to shift the Ed.D. dissertation away from the traditional 5-chapter research project typical of a Ph.D. At that time, Ed.D. students had three formatting options from which to choose: action research, program evaluation, or policy reports. According to meeting minutes from September 2011, the Coordinating Committee shared thoughts and concerns related to changing the dissertation format, including emphasizing the recommendations of CPED to reconsider Ed.D. dissertations as dissertations-in-practice. While it is evident from these notes that there was some resistance (e.g., concerns about rigor, reputation), several individuals noted ways a different format or structure could benefit students (e.g., the experience of writing articles for publication).

This conversation continued in April 2012, at which point the chair of the Department of Educational Leadership and Policy Analysis (ELPA) reiterated the focus of CPED and recommended modifying the dissertation to be more useful to Ed.D. students. According to meeting minutes, there was further discussion around concerns of rigor and reputation, as well as two additional considerations: Institutional Review Board (IRB) approval processes and faculty preparedness to review alternative formats. By the end of the meeting, the Coordinating Committee established a Professional Practice Dissertation Task Force. The work of this task force moved us more solidly into what Rogers (2003) calls the matching stage of the innovation process, exploring alternative formats of dissertations in practice that balanced rigor and fit for scholar-practitioners by reviewing relevant research (e.g., Archbald, 2008; Olson & Clark, 2009) and attending learning exchanges at CPED convenings (e.g., DeLisi, 2012). There we engaged in conversations with fellow CPED colleagues to learn more about how other member institutions formatted their dissertations-in-practice.

After considering several alternative formats for the dissertation-in-practice, such as group dissertations and participatory action research (PAR), the task force determined that none of these met our needs. The alternatives were either:

1) too restrictive in terms of the types of studies students could engage in (e.g., program evaluation);
2) too problematic when discussed with stakeholders (e.g., group dissertations); and/or,
3) did not provide space for the types of analysis and discussion that we believe are important for doctoral scholars to address (e.g., where does the researcher reflect on how the findings contribute/complement extant literature?, where do specific responses to research questions "go"?)

Thus, in the summer and fall of 2012, we focused on designing a structure that would support "well-designed, applied research with substantial value for informing educational practice" (MacGregor & Fellabaum, 2016, p. 58). The result was an outline of a six-section dissertation-in-practice with intentional focus on problems of practice, context, reflection, and two "ready to go" pieces to share with practitioner and scholarly audiences (e.g., conference presentation and journal article).

We shared this proposed format with the Coordinating Committee and a focus group of alumni in the fall of 2012. The alumni also noted concerns over adherence to rigor and the sustainment of MU's academic reputation. In large part, their concerns related to whether changing the formatting would "water down" the end product, as they believed that the program's reputation was partially tied to the rigorous demands of the dissertation process, something that further served to legitimate their degree in the workplace. However, there was positive feedback regarding the reflection and journal article components. Focus group participants believed that the redesign would address the confusion some students encountered when constructing and formatting dissertations. For example, one focus group participant stated:

> I believe my committee was not well aware of the difference or what research we were taught in my Ed.D., so my dissertation is similar to many of the ELPA Ph.Ds. I do believe there should be some difference, but the focus should continue to be on research and writing in some form. Frankly, I believe this is why some students do

> not finish. They are frustrated by what the focus of the program is versus what the committees believe should be done.

Another concern arose regarding group dissertations. Would adopting them increase complexity, confusion, and the need for additional supports in the dissertation-writing phase? As another focus group participant explained:

> I do think it would be valuable to allow more time in the 2-year coursework to get started on the dissertation. Not all advisors handle the dissertation process the same, which means some get lots of help from advisors, and others get very little.

This reinforced our need to redesign the curriculum and comprehensive examinations to ensure alignment across the program. This work, along with a continued discussion of the proposed dissertation-in-practice model, picked back up in late 2013. Furthermore, one of our Cohort 8 students and their advisor began piloting the proposed structure to determine feasibility and identify potential issues early on.

In the fall of 2013, the Coordinating Committee reviewed the proposed dissertation-in-practice outline and discussed the need for indicators or further description within each section. The Coordinating Committee also noted the importance of ensuring that students, advisors, and doctoral committees understood the new design and recognized the benefits for students. The Coordinating Committee charged the task force with developing additional details for the proposed dissertation-in-practice outline and resources for faculty and students. In December 2013, the task force met to work through each section in the new dissertation-in-practice outline, identifying ways to provide additional clarity and guidance around expectations. We also had the opportunity to learn from students piloting the proposed model—how they approached each section, their various titles, content, what worked, and what did not work. For example, in Section Two (initially titled *Context for Study - Setting*), the students shared that they found it easier to weave the history/background of the organization into the discussion of the context. In the end, we retitled the section, which became *Practitioner Setting for the Study* with guidance for students to address the history of the organization (e.g., background) before moving into organizational and leadership analyses. The students also shared what course resources were helpful in preparing this section (e.g., readings from *Harvard Business Review*).

When the task force next met on January 31, 2014, it shared the dissertation-in-practice outline with the Coordinating Committee, who brainstormed revisions to the comprehensive exams. The task force also developed two potential models for the Coordinating Committee to consider: 1) a three-paper structure to include a leadership statement, connection statement, and research prospectus; or, 2) a two-paper structure to include a leadership statement and a research prospectus. In light of the proposed redesign of the dissertation-in-practice, Coordinating Committee members recognized the usefulness of the two-paper structure as it contributed directly to preparing students for their dissertation-in-practice proposal. However, there were concerns that this shift would take away the opportunities the three-paper structure (which was more similar to what was done previously) provided students to reflect on their coursework and make connections. Given the importance role reflection plays throughout the program, the need to keep those reflective components in the comprehensive exam process was evident from our discussions.

The January 2014 meeting also devoted time to continuing discussions of curriculum, identifying where to embed opportunities for students to explore the types of writing found in the dissertation-in-practice. For example, in the *Educational Planning and Evaluation* course, could students produce a practitioner-focused evaluation report? In the companion course, *Data Reporting*, could students produce a scholarly document on the same project (e.g., utilizing a journal structure)? As the group continued its work, one partner institution shared the proposed dissertation-in-practice outline with their current cohort, seeking to identify where the proposed model lacked clarity. For example, students asked about faculty expectations for length within various headings and subheadings within the proposed outline. These discussions proved beneficial, as students realized that length and content would vary based on their particular study. Furthermore, students began to recognize the upcoming shift from most assignments/work in the program being collaborative and highly structured to the dissertation-in-practice, which is much more individually focused work. Additional questions the students shared through this activity included:

- Does the Section Five: Contribution to Scholarship have to be a journal article?
- How detailed do we need to be about assumptions for the study?
- How far back should we go in our explanation of the background of the study?
- What happens if you propose to work with multiple organizations?

The questions shared by students, along with feedback from faculty advising the student piloting the model, served as the foundation for the initial discussion at the April 2014 meeting, giving the redesign task force some final insights to incorporate into the outline (officially finalized for this round in June 2014). Furthermore, the questions informed decision-making for future training and informational sessions (e.g., identifying an appropriate journal for their study).

At this point, the conversation turned to the comprehensive exams with the Coordinating Committee agreeing upon a variation to the proposed three-paper model discussed previously: a research prospectus, an introduction to scholarly review papers connecting directly to the dissertation-in-practice model, and the leadership development paper as an opportunity to engage in reflective practice, including on how the Ed.D. Program curriculum has influenced them as educational leaders. We then continued our discussions of the curriculum for 2014–2015, seeking to identify in which courses the scaffolding of these revisions should take place. The final portion of this 2-day Coordinating Committee meeting focused on strategic planning, addressing the question: What should Ed.D. graduates be able to do, and what should they know? In this discussion, we intentionally referenced the CPED design concepts and principles so that our language aligned when appropriate. What emerged were programmatic learning objectives we developed and still utilized (with only minor edits) 8 years later (see Table 2.1).

Table 2.1. MU Ed.D. Programmatic Learning Objectives

Graduates will know	Graduates will be able to
The importance of being responsive to issues of social justice, including power, privilege, and difference.	Work collaboratively to achieve organizational goals with a variety of individuals.
How to identify problems of practice.	Provide effective leadership to their respective organizations.
The value of reflective practice.	Address problems of practice through the use of pre-existing and collection of data.
Theories and research behind teams and group dynamics.	Engage in reflective practice.
	Respond to issues of social justice within their organizations and communities.

The final pieces of programmatic revision for this cycle took place in the remainder of 2014 through 2015. This included adjustments to our admissions process as well as our vision and mission statements. Our admissions process had always involved two steps, an initial screening to identify applicants to invite for Interview Day, during which candidates completed writing and problem-solving activities and participated in interviews by pairs of faculty and/or alumni. Candidates had completed two separate writing and problem-solving activities, asking them to share their thoughts on team versus individual decision-making and to respond to a case. Beginning with Cohort 10 (spring 2015), we combined these two activities into one, asking candidates to review a case and respond to specific questions adapted from Vaccaro et al. (2013), such as, What will be your strategy for dealing with unforeseen issues, unintended consequences, or problems related to the implementation of your plan?

While using a case was not new to our process, we became intentional, selecting cases that included ethical issues around diversity, requiring organizational change. We believe this shift allowed us to get a better sense of how applicants might approach leadership, change, ethical issues of diversity, and collaboration, directly influenced by CPED principles and in dialogue with other member institutions. Finally, in October 2015 we updated our vision and mission statements:

- The vision is to create scholarly practitioners who transform educational policies, programs, and practices through ethical and compassionate leadership.
- The mission is to enhance the knowledge and competencies of educational leaders who provide optimal conditions for the education of all learners.

Applying for the 2017 Program of the Year Award

When CPED announced the call for applications for the inaugural POY award, we saw a chance to reflect upon the strengths of the Ed.D. Program and the work done in preceding years to incorporate CPED principles and concepts. Since the beginning of our program, our Ed.D. students have been researching problems of practice within their localized contexts. We simply lacked the common language that CPED provided to describe and represent these studies. Providing time and space for stakeholder input enabled us to respond to concerns about the impacts on rigor and reputation we encountered during the restructuring process. It also gave stakeholders a chance to learn about the CPED framework and professional practice programs outside of education (e.g., nursing). Our persistent messaging that restructuring served as a way to improve intentionality in how the information is organized in a dissertation-in-practice and had very little to do with making any changes in the actual process of completing a dissertation-in-practice.

Once invited to submit a full application for the POY in spring 2017, we reached out to faculty, students, and alumni of Cohorts 7–9 (those most likely to be aware of the influence of CPED at that time), asking them to share their experiences in the program. We asked them specifically about the quality of the curriculum, the responsiveness of the program, and the impact of the program and the dissertation-in-practice. Regarding the curriculum and CPED principles and design concepts, one stated:

> Starting with the first semester of classwork (Summer 1), course work included addressing the Problem of Practice. As Scholarly Practitioners, we know how to use the tools available to solve

> problems of practice. The Wicked Problem activities and related assignments provide students with the practice of tackling the biggest problems. In addition, students are asked to identify and address problems of practice in their own work. Each semester students are able to practice the professional skills, grounded in theory, to build competence.

When we asked alumni to describe the impact of the dissertation-in-practice, they talked about impact on self, organizations, policy, communities, and scholarship. Here are a few examples:

- My dissertation was both personally and professionally empowering. The subject matter was not only cathartic and culturally relevant to me, it has proven beneficial in starting conversations in my organization about equity, social identity development, and identity expression.
- I am now in the second resubmission phase to an international journal. Although it has been very challenging, I have continued to pursue publication. The support of my advisor . . . has continued well past my graduation date. It is exciting to think that my dissertation will not just sit on a shelf, but possibly be published. This validates all of my hard work over the years.

The award application process was itself of great benefit, as it afforded us the opportunity to engage in systematic reflection on our impact, our program's distinctiveness, and the influence of CPED on our Ed.D. program. Perhaps one of the most valuable aspects was identifying the positive impacts faculty shared. Several faculty spoke to the impact of the program and increased opportunities to publish and present with their advisees because of the programmatic changes. For example, one faculty member stated:

- The faculty participating in the program have grown professionally and personally as a result of the program. Faculty members have learned from one another, have conducted research and published together, and have become close colleagues who are committed to the program and its outcomes. Student evaluations of the program have routinely demonstrated how the program

> has changed students and in turn the organizations for which they provide leadership. Graduates of the program have become superintendents, deans, and vice presidents, and have occupied other positions of leadership throughout the state of Missouri. As a consequence, this program has had a major impact on education in Missouri and beyond.

As the recipient of CPED's inaugural Program of the Year Award, we were elated knowing our continuous improvement efforts received recognition. Adding to the poignancy, the award coincided with our celebrations of the 20th anniversary of the Statewide Cooperative Ed.D. Program.

Coda: Post-Award Innovations

In the fall of 2019, we shared information with the Coordinating Committee regarding a projected financial deficit facing the Statewide Cooperative Ed.D. Program. This was in response to proposed changes to MU's budget model and reductions in program resources, including budget cuts of 10% to 12% in each of the 2 years prior. At the September 2019 and February 2020 Coordinating Committee meetings, the group brainstormed ideas to reduce expenses and increase revenues. The approved measures included applying for an increase in tuition, admitting 10 additional students per cohort, removing cohort picnics during Summer 2, and reducing the number of summer graduate assistants. We also discussed ways to reduce costs associated with Interview Day. Unfortunately, soon after these discussions, the COVID-19 pandemic created additional financial instability. Facing significant budget cuts, we opted to suspend enrollment and focus on matriculating existing students successfully.

We convened a task force comprised of faculty members in the fall of 2020 to discuss redesigning the Ed.D. from a statewide cooperative program to a single-institution program at MU. Discussions began with an openness to innovation and new possibilities, including potential partnerships with other existing degrees (e.g., Ph.D., Ed.S.) and other departments within the college. This initial conversation led us to establish core elements we wanted to see in our redesign, including that the new Ed.D. be a 3-year program with a set curriculum of 54 credit hours, online (synchronous and asynchronous), and continuing the part-time cohort model. We also wanted to highlight a key strength of our program, which is that we approach education from a blended PK20+ perspective.

The initial clarity and consensus about these elements created some momentum for unknown or uncertain elements, including the approvals necessary for any proposed program changes, funding, and the number of students needed to make the program feasible. We reviewed materials collected via CPED convenings, the CPED website, and corresponded with similar institutional profiles as MU or innovative institutions (e.g., Vanderbilt, University of Maryland, and William & Mary). A staff member examined CPED member institutions' website, creating a spreadsheet outlining key features of each program:

- Do they have a cohort-based model?
- How long do they state it will take to complete their program?
- What is the total number of credit hours required and the breakdown by coursework vs. dissertation/capstone?
- What kind of dissertation/capstone do they require?
- What is the focus of their program?
- What information is available regarding their admission process?
- How many students do they accept?
- When does the application cycle begin?
- Is the program fully online?
- Is the GRE required?
- What other information might be of interest?

In the task force's second meeting in October 2020, we drew upon our network of current Ed.D. students and alumni to learn what they appreciated most about the program, what was least beneficial, and what could have been emphasized. We also asked about their dissertation-in-practice process, including how prepared they felt, their preferences around methods, and the limitations/benefits of the current dissertation-in-practice model. Finally, we asked for their ideas about a new Ed.D. program within a post-COVID context. The November 2020 meeting then focused on the structure of the Ed.D. and options related to coursework and timing. As an award-winning program, we felt confident about program structure and quality. However, we were amenable modifying the curriculum according to student and faculty feedback.

To make a 3-year program feasible, we wanted the dissertation-in-practice embedded in coursework during Years 2 and 3. Many other questions emerged at this time, such as:

- Should methodology courses focus on specific methodologies (e.g., case study)?
- Should courses run from fall through summer or summer through spring?
- Should the third-year focus only on dissertation-in-practice work?
- How might we scaffold dissertation advising into the coursework?
- How might we streamline the dissertation-in-practice to reduce redundancy?

Another November 2020 meeting focused on the results of a survey administered to current students and alumni. The key themes affirmed that most preferred the cohort and PK20+ approach to the program. Respondents suggested fewer group projects and more focus on individual practice problems. At this meeting, we considered potential connections between the Ed.D. and the Ed.S. degrees, where students pursuing both degrees could diverge in their coursework in their second year, and Ed.S. students could substitute two courses that would allow them to pursue both degrees simultaneously. Other ideas that emerged from this meeting included:

- offering electives in the second year
- asking emeritus/faculty about their interest in advising
- creating dissertation-in-practice mentors
- considering adjunct faculty support
- encouraging students to pursue specific types of studies (e.g., case study, program evaluation)
- delivery options for courses

- providing graduate teaching assistantships
- marketing to highlight pillars of the program
- suggesting changes to doctoral committees (e.g., two members based in practice), and
- considering increased cohort sizes.

The culminating proposal from the task force communicated the need to redesign the Ed.D. program because the statewide cooperative program was not financially viable. We confirmed our commitment to current students and faculty at partner institutions who would continue to support those students. We noted the substantial interest from prospective students, identifying 120 potential applicants for the newly redesigned program and over 500 contacts from previous inquiries. The proposal was to implement the revised program in fall 2021 with an application deadline of June 1, 2021 for the first cohort, with plans to move the deadline earlier for subsequent cohorts.

The proposal also identified existing program elements to maintain within the redesigned program. These included:

1. Our PK20+ approach to educational leadership;
2. A focus on serving full-time educational leaders pursuing their doctoral work part-time;
3. A cohort model that builds personal and professional networks;
4. An every other year admissions cycle; and,
5. Curriculum focused on connections between theory and practice and an ability to solve complex problems in educational settings across the critical lenses of leadership, organizations, policy, and the content and context of learning, culminating in the dissertation-in-practice.

We also identified four primary major changes from the statewide model, with the starkest difference being the transition to a single institution program run solely through MU. The second change was to remove the in-person summer requirement and face-to-face instruction at instructional sites around the state during the fall and spring terms. This change addressed the increasing interest we received for the program beyond the state of Missouri. A third change involved increasing the total credit hours from 46 to 54. The former iteration of the program involved a mix of courses ranging from 1 to 4 credit hours, and the program plans required a different number of total credits each semester. The proposed redesign would allow for a standard 6 credit hours each semester (fall, spring, summer), at two 3-credit hour courses each semester for nine semesters. This increase reflected the added programmatic support that students would need in completing dissertations-in-practice and alignment with other CPED-influenced Ed.D. programs nationally. The fourth primary change was to the comprehensive examination requirements. Given the curricular changes, the faculty wanted to transition students more directly from the coursework into their dissertation-in-practice. Thus, the comprehensive examination requirements went from a three-paper model to a dissertation-in-practice proposal.

With any major programmatic changes, there are growing pains and tension points requiring additional clarifications or adjustments. Thus far, we have identified three major clarifications now that the first and second cohorts of the redesigned program are underway. The first clarification was regarding the ebb and flow of the biennial nature of the Ed.D. program. Consistent with previous cohorts, our plan is to enroll larger cohorts every other year. Specifically, our first cohort of the redesigned Ed.D. was large by design with an enrollment goal of 60 students. This partially addressed a backlog of interested applicants that far exceeded this cohort size. However, faculty quickly grew concerned about our capacity to properly advise 60 students working on their dissertation-in-practices during their third year (and every other year subsequently). Prior to soliciting applications for the second cohort, the faculty voted to move to annual cohorts of 30 students. The rationale for this change was to smooth the advising and committee work across every year (30 dissertations each year) rather than having alternating years of extensive dissertation work (60 dissertations vs. 0 dissertations every other year). A secondary benefit of this change was that prospective students would not have to wait 2 years to apply.

The second clarification was to address faculty concerns about advising loads by offering a revised dissertation-in-practice. The new outline complies with CPED guidelines while also more closely mirroring a journal article format, which we hope will make it more likely for students to be able to publish their work. Specifically, the revised dissertation-in-practice model consists of seven sections. The first six sections closely resemble a typical journal article: introduction, literature review, conceptual/theoretical framework, methodology, findings, and discussion. The seventh section, scholarly practitioner reflection, requires the students to reflect on how their research can influence practice.

Upon launching the redesigned Ed.D. program in fall 2021, the faculty realized we needed to rethink advising. For previous cohorts, students were assigned advisors with an aim to equitably share the advising load and to match student and faculty interests as best possible. We were distributing 18 to 20 students across 10 to 12 faculty every other year. At an average Ed.D. advising load of roughly two students per faculty, the work was considered part of a normal advising load with no special considerations within our assigned workload. Under the initially redesigned Ed.D. model, we would distribute 60 students across eight eligible faculty. The faculty agreed to move towards a group-based advising model where fewer faculty advised a larger number of students. For the first cohort of 60, four faculty will be the primary advisors to 15 students. In subsequent cohorts of 30, two faculty will be the primary advisors. During each of the final four semesters of a student's program, they will register for six credits of coursework with their primary advisor. The advising faculty receive compensation for their work during the two summer semesters and receive credit for two courses during the academic year. By formally integrating Ed.D. advising into a faculty's workload, the faculty are better able to focus on the success of the students and offer feedback just as they would with regular courses.

Three Key Lessons Learned

In closing, we want to review three key lessons learned through these cycles of innovation. The first is that time spent building and nurturing a culture of continuous improvement is always time well spent. For example, when concerns emerged regarding components such as rigor or programmatic reputation, program leaders were able to continue to move the conversation forward by being prepared with data and arguments that highlighted what Rogers (2003) refers to as compatibility. For Rogers, compatibility is defined as "the degree to which an innovation is perceived as consistent with the existing values, past experiences, and needs of potential adopters" (p. 240). Compatibility was often at the core of the discussions we had with other Ed.D. programs who contacted us to learn more after we received the POY award. In addition, Rogers' concept of observability was important to colleagues in these discussions, as it was to our own internal discussions when we were exploring what options we might consider. Rogers defines observability as "the degree to which the results of an innovation are visible to others" (p. 258). In other words, proof of concept goes a long way when engaged in a cycle of innovation.

Second, we found stakeholder groups were much more willing to consider changes when they recognized the extent to which we had explored potential options—what Rogers (2003) referred to as relative advantage, which is "the degree to which an innovation is perceived as being better than the idea it supersedes" (p. 229). Relative advantage was not only important when redesigning the dissertation-in-practice (and the other major programmatic components, prior to winning the award); this was also important to highlight when communicating the decision to close the Statewide Cooperative Ed.D. Program and relaunch a revised program.

This brings us to the third and final lesson. Even when you have an award-winning program, contextual factors beyond your control will sometimes require major changes. In our case, changes in institutional finances emerged as a driving factor. As the process of closing the Statewide Cooperative Ed.D. Program began, we considered the feasibility of redesigning the program in order to admit a new cohort beginning coursework in fall 2021. This included:

- identifying faculty with the capacity and interest to be a part of the 2020 redesign task force;

- working with the Provost Office and Academic Affairs at MU System to learn about the process of submitting program changes for review; and,
- designing a timeline that accounted for stakeholder involvement and identifying potential options (i.e., becoming a 3-year program).

Once the task force was underway in late summer/early fall 2020, the concepts of trialability and complexity (Rogers, 2003) rose to the fore of our process. Rogers (2003) defines trialability as "the degree to which an innovation may be experimented with on a limited basis" (pp. 257–258) and complexity as "the degree to which an innovation is perceived as relatively difficult to understand or use" (p. 257). We benefitted from a strong foundation to build upon—an award-winning program aligned with CPED principles. Furthermore, our program strongly values continuous improvement and stakeholder involvement. Our current students, alumni, and program faculty identified features that needed to stay the same (e.g., PK-20+ perspective, curricular lenses) and features needing change (e.g., expected time to degree, embedding dissertation-in-practice work even further into the curriculum). Thus, as we explored what other Ed.D. programs at CPED institutions were doing, we identified concepts/components of interest, with a timeline and capacity in mind.

In fall 2020, the task force decided to maintain the current dissertation-in-practice structure, as we determined that the primary models of interest (e.g., designing a change-oriented project that involved clients as an option for students in nonprofits) were less triable and more complex. Finally, after the first cohort of the revised Ed.D. program was admitted in fall 2021, the faculty embodied Rogers' concept of trialability with the dissertation-in-practice model, "re-inventing it so as to customize it more closely to the individual's [or program's] conditions" (p. 258).

Endnotes

1. When we refer to PK20+ perspective in our Ed.D. Program, we are referencing our focus on educational leadership across the lifespan. While the majority of our students tend to work in PK–12 or Higher Education, we regularly have a number of students whose work falls into areas better defined as educational leadership within communities, corporations, medicine, nonprofits, and so forth.
2. See Mountford (2005) for a description of that redesign process.

References

Archbald, D. (2008). Research versus problem solving for the education leadership doctoral thesis: Implications for form and function. *Educational Administration Quarterly, 44*(5), 704–739. https://doi.org/10.1177/0013161X07313288

DeLisi, R. (2012, June 28). *University descriptions of professional practice doctorates: Next steps for CPED.* Presented at the June Convening of the Carnegie Project on the Education Doctorate, Fresno, California.

MacGregor, C. J., & Fellabaum, J. (2016). Dissertation redesign for scholarly practitioners in educational leadership: Increasing impact through dissemination-ready sections. In V. A. Storey & K. A. Hesbol (Eds.), *Contemporary approaches to dissertation development and research methods* (pp. 53–69). Information Science Reference.

Mountford, M. (2005). The journey toward transformational learning in a statewide doctoral program. *Innovative Higher Education, 30*(3), 213–227. https://doi.org/10.1007/s10755-005-6305-4

Olson, K., & Clark, C. M. (2009). A signature pedagogy in doctoral education: The leader-scholar community. *Educational Researcher, 38*(3), 216–221. https://doi.org/10.3102/0013189X09334207

Rogers, E. M. (2003). Diffusion of innovations (eBook edition). Free Press.

Vaccaro, A., McCoy, B., Champagne, D., & Siegel, M. (2013). *Decisions matter: Using a decision-making framework with contemporary student affairs case studies.* NASPA - Student Affairs Administrators in Higher Education.

CHAPTER THREE

Arizona State University's Ed.D. in Leadership and Innovation—An Award-Winning Ed.D. Program at Scale

RAY R. BUSS AND JOSEPHINE P. MARSH

Our decision to seek the CPED Program of the Year Award for Arizona State University's Ed.D. in Leadership and Innovation was based on the premise that our program had several innovative signature pedagogies (Carnegie Project on the Education Doctorate [CPED], n.d.; Shulman, 2005; Shulman et al., 2006) valuable to students during the program (Buss, 2020; Buss & Allen, 2020; Buss & Avery, 2017) and to graduates after they completed the program (Buss, 2019; Mertler, 2023). Specifically, we considered that our two signature pedagogies—the use of cycles of action research (CARs) throughout the program and leader scholar communities (LSCs) during the dissertation phase—warranted dissemination because these approaches fostered students' successes. Because of the comprehensive nature of these signature pedagogies, which sought to support students' learning of appropriate research skills for their workplaces and completing the dissertation and program in a timely manner, we believed these pedagogies would be useful for other Ed.D. programs.

Founded in 1885 as the Territorial Normal School, Arizona State University (ASU) has a rich history of developing highly qualified teachers and educational leaders. It has since emerged as a doctoral university with very high research activity over the last 30-plus years. Recently, consistent with its Charter, ASU has achieved recognition for its vision as the "New American University" (Crow & Dabars, 2015), leading the way in innovation, providing access to all, demonstrating excellence in research and teaching, and having a positive impact on the communities it serves. In 2023, the Association of American Universities invited ASU to join the association of universities that serve as national leaders in research and academics. Throughout the history of the institution, a strong, nationally recognized College of Education has been present, most recently as Mary Lou Fulton Teachers College. It provides a broad range of quality programs, including undergraduate programs leading to teacher certification, well-recognized master's degree programs in a variety of educational disciplinary areas, and notably, doctoral programs that have achieved and maintained high national reputations.

Our award-winning Ed.D. program was developed between 2004 and 2006. The mission of the program has been focused on developing *scholarly and influential practitioners*, those who lead, innovate, collaborate, and conduct research appropriate to their workplace settings. Further, the program was designed to equip leaders with the knowledge, skills, and dispositions to resolve problems of practice and improve their local educational contexts. As a charter member of CPED, faculty members have aligned the program with CPED guiding principles, such as focusing on equity and diversity, preparing leaders to make a positive difference in their settings, and affording field-based opportunities to work on their "problem of practice" ([PoP]; Buss, 2018a). Additionally, CPED design features such as focusing on a PoP, employing signature pedagogies, implementing inquiry as practice, and requiring a dissertation-in-practice guided the program.

Each student in Arizona State University's Ed.D. in Leadership and Innovation program comes with a complex PoP, a key CPED design feature (CPED, n.d.). Many of the PoPs have reflected *diversity and equity* issues in their communities, thus aligning with CPED guiding principle #1 (CPED, n.d.). For example, teachers from K–12 schools have focused on PoPs dealing with equity issues. These include improving instruction for English language learners and providing equitable learning experiences. Students working in higher education have been concerned with equity issues such as supporting first-generation college students, providing equity for students of color, and enhancing the retention or transfer of students. The program mission aligns with CPED guiding principle #2, which stated Ed.D. programs should "prepare leaders who can construct and apply knowledge to make a positive difference in the lives of individuals, families, organizations, and communities" (CPED, n.d., para. 2). With respect to CPED principle #3, our Ed.D. program has afforded opportunities for students to collaborate with diverse communities and build partnerships, which have been essential as students conduct ongoing action research throughout the program including the dissertation-in-practice.

Consistent with CPED principle #4, students have focused their efforts in workplace settings as they explored and attempted to resolve their PoP by engaging in CARs (Buss, 2018b). As students worked on their PoP, they grounded their efforts in a professional knowledge base that integrated practical and research knowledge by linking theory with systematic inquiry, CPED principle #5, during the execution of their CARs. Finally, with respect to principle #6, students have generated, transformed, and employed professional knowledge and practice to aid in the resolution of their PoP.

In all, the 60-hour doctoral portion of the program (30 hours of a required master's degree are accepted as part of the 90-hour program) has included several areas of coursework such as a professional core, a research core, advanced professional studies, and research and dissertation hours. The culmination of the program has been a *dissertation in practice*, a CPED design feature, based on their PoP. LSCs, a *signature pedagogy* in our program, have been used to facilitate students' work and completion of the research and dissertation portion of the program (Buss, 2022; Buss & Allen, 2020).

The first cohort of students was admitted in 2006 and graduated in 2009. To this point, the program has graduated about 360 students. Originally, the program provided coursework and dissertation support for 60 students. Over the last 3 years, we have increased our total enrollment to around 300. Because we needed to scale the program up quickly, including offering numerous class sections, expanding support of dissertation work, and increasing student services, we have worked to continuously improve and adapt the program and its delivery, which we discuss in the following sections of the chapter.

Ed.D. in Leadership and Innovation: Its Origins, Journey, and Signature Pedagogies

In this section, we discuss our work on *agenda setting* and *matching* efforts as we sought innovations to solve two concerns that arose as we were developing our Ed.D. program. Rogers (1995) asserted that agenda setting occurs when there is an organizational problem identified as in need of attention and a solution. Moreover, we describe our efforts at matching, what Rogers (1995) defined as fitting an innovation to a problem in our organization's agenda. Efforts during these two stages resulted in the development of two innovations. From our program perspective, an innovation is a new method, idea, or process that enhances student learning or participation in the program. Thus, our innovations have become our signature pedagogies—CARs and LSCs.

As we were developing our program, two crucial concerns arose among the faculty members tasked with designing the program. The first was how to incorporate an approach to research that was practical and practicable for professionals working on a full-time basis while taking coursework and conducting research in their workplace settings. After considerable thought, discussion, and early implementation with adjustments, program faculty members made some modifications and settled on implementing the program's research approach using CARs, the first of the program's two innovations to resolve this concern. The program faculty embedded CARs strategically throughout coursework during the first 2 years of the program (see Buss, 2018b). In their action research, students develop an action research concept paper and then engage in reconnaissance in their workplace settings as an initial, action research cycle. Subsequently, they conduct several CARs involving small-scale interventions, instrument development, revision, and so on.

The second concern that arose among faculty members designing the program focused on how to ensure students completed their dissertation work in a timely way. Ample evidence has shown the dissertation has tended to be a stumbling block for many doctoral students (Lovitts, 2001; Walker et al., 2008). Generally, students received strong support during their doctoral coursework but found the dissertation work to be less structured, requiring more individualized attention, and resulting in approximately 50% of students who do not complete doctoral programs (Bowen & Rudenstine, 1992; Ivankova & Stick, 2007). To avoid student isolation and attrition and to support our students' dissertation efforts, we considered and developed LSCs, which offered academic, professional, and emotional support (Buss, 2022; Buss & Allen, 2020).

We assigned one faculty member to each community of five to seven students. This faculty member served as their LSC chair and worked closely with them during the students' last 2 years of the program, guiding and mentoring them through the dissertation-in-practice process. Over the course of the final four semesters, LSCs met regularly as students developed an action research plan; composed and defended a dissertation proposal; implemented their innovation/intervention while collecting data; analyzed the data; and finalized and defended their dissertation-in-practice. For campus-based cohorts, LSCs met regularly in person, whereas online cohorts met virtually on a consistent basis. They also provided opportunities within the LSCs to sustain the community already established in students' larger cohorts and build closer relationships among and between the students and themselves (Buss & Graves Wolf, 2021). Work with LSCs counted as a course, with students receiving research and dissertation course credits and faculty members including it as part of their teaching workload each of the four semesters. We viewed the LSCs as an innovation implemented by the program to provide academic, professional, and emotional support during the four-semester dissertation process (Buss, 2022; Buss & Allen, 2020). In fact, once students enrolled in LSCs, 92% of them completed their dissertations in the four semesters of LSC and thus completed the program in the expected 3-year timeframe.

We received the CPED Outstanding Program Award in 2018 when our program consisted of 180 students, with 120 of those in LSCs, including one face-to-face and two online cohorts. Subsequently, about eight new LSCs were established each year. LSC chairs were typically involved in the program as instructors and/or had been involved in designing the program. They understood the goals of the program, were committed to the program's success, and possessed the vision for how LSCs might support students' dissertation efforts. Given the size of the program at that time, LSC chairs could and did meet in one room to discuss issues arising from the implementation of LSCs, including what was working and what needed to be refined to ensure effective efforts in the LSCs.

A New Need: Redefining/Restructuring, Clarifying, and Routinizing the Innovations

After we received the award, our online program began to expand and in spring of 2020 grew unexpectedly. Typically, we admitted one cohort of 20 each term: spring, summer, and fall. Instead, we admitted three online cohorts of 20 in that spring semester, one campus-based cohort in the summer, and two online cohorts the following fall. This was due to exceptionally strong applicant pools and ASU's commitment to admitting all qualified students into our programs, as well as the addition of special cohorts—one international cohort of 20 and one cohort of seven students, which increased the size of our regular cohorts. Exceptional growth continued the following fall and spring and this level of program implementation with concomitant increasing student participation continues to the present day. Notably, our program has been aligned with ASU's commitment that universities should be measured *not* by whom they exclude, but by whom they include and how they support those students to attain success (ASU Charter, Mission, & Goals, n.d.). Thus, we were encouraged to expand the program while finding ways to support our students academically, professionally, and emotionally, as well as our faculty members who took on the responsibilities of working with larger numbers of students. We have firmly believed and continue to believe the implementation of LSCs is an effective innovation that provides these supports. Evidence from a recent study corroborated this perspective (Buss, 2022), revealing that students described their LSCs as being beneficial by (a) affording support in academic, social, and emotional areas, (b) providing supportive functions like accountability, communicating information, and feedback, and (c) developing self-generated, informal approaches like monitoring progress and sharing information or strategies to support one another.

During the 2021–2022 academic year, we created 19 new LSCs, a significant increase from the eight LSCs typical in previous years. Although the number of new LSC chairs decreased slightly the following academic year, our need still has been much greater than it had been in the past and much greater than the number needed in the original program design. This required recruiting many more faculty members to be chairs. Unlike the original LSC chairs who had been intimately involved in designing this structure, almost all of these recruited faculty members had never been involved in the program at all. They lacked knowledge of the program's mission, its goals of developing scholarly and influential practitioners, and the expectations of the LSC experience. They had not been part of conversations about LSCs previously, so were unaware of the expectations of the LSC experience. Nor had they experienced the culture we expected LSC chairs to nurture throughout the LSC experience. Although many of the faculty members had mentored Ph.D. students through the typical dissertation experience, most had never mentored students through an action research dissertation process. Further, they had not provided the kinds of support we expected chairs to provide students so they would complete their action research dissertation-in-practice on time. In short, they had not been socialized into the program or the role of LSC chair.

We found ourselves faced with our own urgent problem of practice. How could we maintain the core values, mission, and expectations of the program and the intent of what we believed were our most powerful signature pedagogies—action research cycles and the LSC—as we grew to meet the needs of students and the expectations of the college and university? This challenge offered an opportunity to *redefine/restructure* our innovations, *clarify* our innovations, and *routinize* them. These last three steps of the innovation process *within* an organization (Rogers, 1995) allowed us to refine and more fully disseminate the innovations to faculty members throughout the organization (i.e., our program and college). Per Rogers (1995), "*Redefining/restructuring* occurs when the innovation is re-invented to accommodate the organization's needs and structure more closely, and when the organization's structure is modified to fit with the innovation" (p. 394, italics in original). Redefining/restructuring was certainly appropriate for our organization because we needed to modify the organization's structure to provide for wider dissemination of the innovation within the organization. In clarifying an innovation, Rogers maintains that clarifying occurs when members of an organization use an innovation more widely, becoming clearer to members of the organization. Certainly, our efforts required us to clarify the innovations for our newly participating faculty members. Finally, Rogers suggested *routinization* occurs when the innovation becomes a part of the organization's ongoing activities and loses a bit of its unique identity as being an innovation. Our efforts in this area have been ongoing as we have continued to share the innovations with other faculty members.

Cycles of Action Research and a Growing Program

As we grew, new faculty members needed to develop an understanding of the program's core values, mission, and expectations and how they related to the signature pedagogies. We understood that this would not occur through a single day of orientation or by reading program guides. It would take an extended amount of time and interaction among and between students and faculty. We needed to socialize faculty members into the program at the same time they were teaching and mentoring students in the program.

As we added additional course sections to accommodate increasing enrollments, we took two actions to ensure fidelity of program implementation of the CAR processes across all sections. First, we carefully aligned the CAR process across the program's semesters, describing each research cycle in detail to ensure students and instructors were clear on the expectations (Buss, 2018b). Furthermore, we developed a graphic, which we revised over time, visually depicting when cycles of research would take place and the kinds of research activities conducted on a semester basis to add further clarification.

Second, course coordinators created instructional guides that were shared with all instructors teaching the sections of these courses. The instructional guides offered information about the course content, areas where students might experience difficulty, instructions related to grading and providing substantive feedback, notes from previous semesters, and so on, to assist those teaching these courses. For courses connected to the action research process, additional notes related to CAR were included in these guides.

Course coordinators also began meeting regularly with instructors to support them as they guided students through course content and appropriate CAR. Each semester, the program began holding instructor meetings. Agenda items included the importance of CAR to the program and how these cycles fit into the students' overall research and learning experiences. We explained the success of the students' action research dissertation-in-practice projects often depended on what they learned as they conducted these earlier cycles of action research and shared how the coursework was structured or sequenced to ensure a coherent experience for the students. These meetings have provided instructors with important information about the program and the CAR signature pedagogy.

Leader Scholar Communities and a Growing Program

As noted previously, another of our signature pedagogies has been LSCs. To address our problem of practice to maintain the program's core values, mission, and expectations, meet the needs of a growing program, and socialize faculty into the program, we refined several activities related to LSCs. As part of our response, we modified the annual LSC Chair retreat. What began as an all-day, face-to-face retreat during the summer was changed to a 4-hour Zoom meeting in 2020 due to the COVID-19 pandemic. The goal of these meetings remained the same—focusing on students' dissertation-in-practice journeys. Regardless of their experience level, all LSC chairs were expected to attend the retreat and received a small summer stipend.

Retreat topics included an overview of the program's goals, expectations, and policies; descriptions of the role of chair and committee members; information about action research and what counted as action research in the program; a list of dissertation benchmarks and recommended timelines by semester; and discussions about the content, nature, and processes of LSC meetings. The online retreats have continued and offer many opportunities to share ideas among experienced and new chairs for building community within LSCs and motivating students through the dissertation-in-practice process. New LSC chairs often claimed they left these meetings with information overload and many additional questions.

For years, the LSC Retreat was the only formal informational meeting and training held for LSC chairs. Notably, with the addition of new chairs who were not familiar with the program or dissertation-in-practice, we realized LSC chairs needed additional support. Although some new LSC chairs asked questions of more experienced chairs, others just plowed forward by drawing upon experiences of their own dissertation or from their mentoring of Ph.D. students' dissertations. We often found inconsistencies between how LSC chairs envisioned doctoral dissertation research and how our program defined an action research dissertation-in-practice. To address these inconsistencies, we began holding regular hour-long LSC chair meetings on a routine basis.

We began by holding one Zoom meeting each semester and slowly increased to monthly hour-long meetings. These meetings were not required but have been listed as an expectation for those serving as an LSC chair. Most LSC chairs have attended these meetings. The agenda for each meeting includes time for open discussion and begins with an open-ended prompt such as: How are things going with your LSC? What things are going well with your LSC? What things are causing you concern? Share something that went well in one of your LSC meetings. We also provide program announcements and a presentation and discussion on a specific topic. Topics have ranged from building community, discussing resources available for the online Canvas course shell they can use with their LSC, exploring mentor texts, to providing activities to facilitate LSC meetings. Other topics have included the institutional review board (IRB) process, comprehensive examinations, ideas for guiding students through development of the dissertation, expectations of committee members, and holding proposal and dissertation defenses. Sometimes these meetings are used to solicit information about program needs and additional supports needed for students. The meetings end with break-out sessions for chairs to meet with other chairs whose students are in the same dissertation phase. For example, all chairs facilitating LSC 1: Proposal Development meet as a group and continue to meet together over the four semesters they serve as LSC chairs. The break-out sessions are led by designated, experienced LSC chairs known as *mentor LSC chairs*, and have become a time for sharing and asking each other questions.

In addition to the monthly meetings, designated mentor LSC chairs are available to meet with their LSC chair cohort members individually or on an as-needed basis. For example, one cohort of chairs—new and experienced—met with their mentor LSC chair for scheduled 30-minute biweekly meetings during the first two semesters of LSC work. They discussed how things were going and asked each other process or procedural questions, brainstormed solutions to student problems, and shared successes. They also talked about expectations for LSC meetings and strategies to motivate students to write. We have continued to expand these sorts of supports and have found that communities of practice have been developing among the LSC chairs. Within these communities of practice, new and experienced chairs share strategies and resources, give each other access to their online documents, and blend their ideas to create new supports and documents. A shared Google drive was created for all LSC chairs to store chair-developed resource documents and guides, a living resource center where LSC chairs can search for information and guidance. Further, the folder is linked to the online LSC course shell for easy access and content for the online courses.

Online resources have been and are continually developed and revised for each LSC cohort and chair. Because each semester of the LSC is considered a course, online course shells have been substantially revised to support the growing numbers of faculty member chairs and students. These revisions have included detailed syllabi with course benchmarks, assignment deadlines (e.g., proposal drafts, intervention description drafts), and timelines. Suggested teaching activities and resources are also included in the courses and students turn in their assignments or dissertation drafts online as part of the course. LSC chairs, now referred to as instructor chairs, have recently been asked to use these online course shells to facilitate their LSCs each semester. This has added support for faculty members and students and a more formal way to approach the LSC. Although LSC instructor-chairs are allowed to personalize their syllabi and use the course resources as they wish, this approach has been one way to socialize new instructor-chairs into the process and program.

As we have described, providing opportunities for faculty to learn about the program through teaching guides, LSC resources, instructor meetings, and faculty mentoring has allowed us to disseminate the innovations that we value as a program more fully. By allowing time for faculty members new to the program to ask questions and provide input and feedback on their experiences with the program and their students, we have been able to make refinements that we may not have done otherwise. In short, our growth and our need to socialize more faculty members into the program have offered us opportunities to *redefine/restructure* our innovations, *clarify* our innovations, and *routinize* them.

Coda

In this chapter, we reflected on the development and diffusion of our innovation *within our organization* (Rogers, 2003), which was necessitated by program growth and the concomitant need to orient, prepare, and support additional faculty members working in the program. Notably, we discussed how we have built upon opportunities to redefine/restructure our program's innovations after we were recognized with CPED's Program of the Year Award; how we clarified our innovations for new faculty in the program as we grew; and how our innovations have become routinized.

We described how our innovation process has been a continuous one, one that incorporated slight modifications and clarifications to our innovations as we accommodated growth and the needs and voices of new faculty members, students, and other constituents.

While we socialized with faculty members about our program and its innovations, we also learned from them. We addressed their questions and feedback as we were adapting, adjusting, and redefining our innovations. Thus, we learned the importance of being open to redefining/restructuring and clarifying in order to *routinize* our innovations, i.e., becoming ongoing aspects of our Ed.D. program.

Notably, we also disseminated information about our innovative signature pedagogies beyond our institution to other organizations. These "outward facing" efforts were more consistent with how Rogers (1995) characterized diffusion and adoption of an innovation by others *outside an organization.* Specifically, Rogers suggested diffusion and adoption of innovations comprised four essential components, including (a) the innovation, (b) communication channels, (c) time, and (d) a social system. The innovation must provide a relative advantage; be compatible with the adopters' needs; be concise to provide for ease of adoption; allow for a trial period; and allow for observing others using the innovation. Communication channels must allow for transfer of information from one group to another. Rogers also viewed time as a critical aspect for diffusion and adoption of an innovation because it is necessary to learn of the innovation, discuss it, adopt it, implement it, and evaluate it. Finally, the social system reflected interested individuals at other institutions.

First, we acknowledge that CPED has been a major venue for our dissemination efforts. CPED provided us opportunities (Rogers' [1995] communication channels) within a collegial national community (Rogers' social system) to share about CARs and LSCs at numerous annual convenings, monthly virtual events, and special interest groups. During and after such events, we had informal conversations—virtually and in person—with faculty members from around the country to discuss our innovations. Inquiring individuals often asked specifics about how we incorporated CARs in our coursework and how we created, implemented, and sustained LSCs.

Moreover, as part of our dissemination efforts, program faculty members have published in CPED's peer-reviewed journal *Impacting Education: Journal on Transforming Professional Practice.* For example, in 2021, Buss and Graves Wolf wrote about how LSCs built and sustained community within our program and Buss (2018b) chronicled the use and sustainment of the action research and CARs throughout the program. Notably, Buss and Allen (2020) documented how LSCs, albeit implemented a bit differently, supported Ed.D. students at two different universities. Program faculty members have also published in other journals and presented at non-CPED conferences such as the annual meeting of the American Educational Research Association (AERA) in order to reach a broader audience. Most recently, Mertler (2023) published research drawing on a survey of our graduates who described the long-term effects of CARs and action research.

CPED's Program of the Year Award application process and then winning the award affirmed to us that our program met and perhaps exceeded CPED's guiding and foundational principles. It opened up our program to discussions among ourselves and with other universities. We grew—more students, more faculty members, and more insights. Growth and pride in our program's recognition as an award winner has motivated us to continue to innovate, redefine/restructure, and take the time and effort to clarify our innovation so they became routinized. Exploring our process through Roger's (1995) theory led us to understand more about our innovation process and how we might proceed in our continuous innovation process.

References

Arizona State University. (n.d.). ASU Charter, mission and goals. https://newamericanuniversity.asu.edu/about/asu-charter-mission-and-goals

Bowen, W. G., & Rudenstine, N. L. (1992). *In pursuit of the Ph.D.* Princeton University Press.

Buss, R. R. (2022, April 22). *Supporting Ed.D. students' dissertation efforts using leader scholar communities II.* [Paper presentation]. Annual Meeting of the American Educational Research Association, San Diego, CA.

Buss, R. R. (2020). Exploring the development of students' identities as educational leaders and educational researchers in a professional practice doctoral program. *Studies in Higher Education, 47*(6), 1069–1083. http://dx.doi.org/10.1080/03075079.2020.1836484

Buss, R. R. (2019). Graduates' continuing work as scholarly practitioners after participation in a Carnegie Project on the Education Doctorate guided, Ed.D. program. *International Journal of Doctoral Studies, 14*, 803–817. https://doi.org/10.28945/4451

Buss, R. R. (2018a). How CPED guiding principles and design concepts influenced the development and implementation of an Ed.D. program. *Impacting Education: Journal on Transforming Professional Practice, 3*(2), 40–47. https://doi:.org/10.5195/ie.2018.57

Buss, R. R. (2018b). Using action research as a signature pedagogy to develop Ed.D. students' inquiry as practice skills. *Impacting Education: Journal of Transforming Professional Practice, 3*(1), 23–31. https://doi.org/105195/ie.2018.46

Buss, R. R., & Allen, J. G. (2020). Leader scholar communities: Supporting Ed.D. students' dissertation in practice efforts. *Impacting Education: Journal on Transforming Professional Practice, 5*(3), 1–7. https://doi.org/10.5195/ie.2020.98

Buss, R. R., & Avery, A. (2017). Research becomes you: Cultivating Ed.D. students' identities as educational leader and researchers and a "learning by doing" meta-study. *Journal of Research on Leadership Education, 12*, 273–301. https://doi.org/10.1177/1942775116674463

Buss, R. R., & Graves Wolf, L. (2021). Building and sustaining community in an online Ed.D. program. *Impacting Education: Journal on Transforming Professional Practice, 6*(3), 47–53. https://doi.org/10.5195/ie.2021.192

CPED. (n.d.). *The CPED framework*. Retrieved from https://www.cpedinitiative.org/the-framework

Crow, M. M., & Dabars, W. B. (2015). *Designing the new American university*. Johns Hopkins University Press.

Ivankova, N. V., & Stick, S. L. (2007). Students' persistence in a distributed doctoral program in educational leadership in higher education: A mixed methods study. *Research in Higher Education, 48*(1), 93–135.

Lovitts, B. (2001). *Leaving the ivory tower: The causes and consequences of departure from doctoral study*. Rowman & Littlefield.

Mertler, C. A. (2023). Online Ed.D. program graduates' persistence for engaging in ongoing practitioner research. *Florida Journal of Educational Research, 60*(1), 1–23. Retrieved from https://journals.flvc.org/fjer/article/view/132955

Rogers, E. M. (1995). *Diffusion of innovations* (4th ed.). The Free Press.

Shulman, L. S. (2005). Signature pedagogies in the professions. *Daedalus, 134*(3), 52–59.

Shulman, L. S., Golde, C. M., Bueschel, A. C., & Garabedian, K. J. (2006). Reclaiming education's doctorates: A critique and a proposal. *Educational Researcher, 35*(3), 25–32. https://doi.org/10.3102/0013189X035003025

Walker, G. E., Golde, C. M., Jones, L., Conklin Bueschel, A., & Hutchings, P. (2008). *The formation of scholars: Rethinking doctoral education for the twenty-first century*. Jossey-Bass.

CHAPTER FOUR

The University of Hawai'i's Ed.D. Program in Professional Educational Practice—Voyages of Discovery, Service, and Continuous Improvement

WALTER KAHUMOKU III AND LORI IDETA

Nearly a half-century ago, the first of the major seafaring voyages across the Pacific began a renewal of Polynesian navigational traditions that had been lost for millennia. In March of 1975, the first double-hulled *wa'a* (canoe) named the *Hōkūle'a* sailed from the sacred shores of Kualoa on the island of O'ahu to begin decades of expeditions based on the ancestral wayfinding wisdom and joined with other forces in the re-empowerment of *Kānaka Hawai'i*, the native people of Hawai'i. This seafaring tradition brought to the forefront the critical *nā 'ike*, or knowledges embedded in Native Hawaiian language, customs, knowledge, skills, history, and most importantly, their courage and resilience to traverse thousands of open ocean to these islands we now call home. It inspired "the rebirth of waka (*wa'a* in Hawaiian) in nations like Aotearoa" and the most recent journey, *Mālama Honua*—the circumnavigation of the globe—drew "attention to the need for a more sustainable world" (Spiller et al., 2015, p. xiv).

This chapter is dedicated to the retelling of a similar voyaging narrative. This *mo'olelo* (story) mirrors the identification of key issues and the collection and use of data to continuously tack so that practicing leaders seeking doctorate degrees can discover, grow, improve, and influence the worlds around them. The authors of this chapter have been involved with this program since its conceptual design and became the program's co-directors in 2018. The previous director, Dr. Sarah Twomey, elected to submit for the Carnegie Project on the Education Doctorate's (CPED) Program of the Year award based on years of discussion, advocacy, design, trial (and error), evaluation, and refinement of a social justice leadership program. Although at times nearly shipwrecked by political controversy, four different sets of directors, financial instability, and other challenges, the current University of Hawai'i College of Education's Doctorate in Professional Educational Practice or Ed.D. has not only been recognized as the CPED Program of the Year but was recently recognized by the Association for Advancing Quality in Educator Preparation (AAQEP) as one of the premier programs offered by the University of Hawai'i's College of Education.

Before proceeding, we, the authors of this chapter, are deeply grateful to the program's previous leadership—Dr. Hunter McEwan (Director, 2009–2014), Dr. Jeff Moniz (Director, 2014–2016), Dr. Sarah Twomey (Director, 2016–2018)—for their contributions to this program. Without them, we would not exist today. They, along with a growing network of community partners who in turn have been instructors, advisors, and mentors, have collectively dealt with each programmatic issue that arose such that the current cohort of students—Cohort IV—have experienced a much more refined set of courses and increased academic and financial supports. Many of the improvements are the results of these leaders.

The chapter presents an overview of the current program and a discussion of four major programmatic problems of practice—identification, data confirmation, short-term improvement pilots, and longer-term program refinements. Since the first cohort's start in 2011, this Ed.D. has served four cohorts of students (see Table 4.1).

The Ed.D. in Professional Educational Practice at the University of Hawai'i at Manoa

The exploration of thousands of miles throughout the Pacific by Indigenous island people is an appropriate metaphor for this Ed.D.'s

Table 4.1. Cohorts of Ed.D. Students at the University of Hawai‘i

Cohort	Year	Number of Students	Program Completers % (Number)
Cohort 1	2011–2014	30	90% (27)
Cohort 2	2014–2017	27	96% (26)
Cohort 3	2017–2020	29	62% (18)
Cohort 4	2020–2023	26	In Progress

Note: Typically, the program welcomes a cohort of students every 3.5 years, and at the time of writing this chapter, the program faculty are completing the admissions process for its fifth cohort.

expedition. This program is part of a College of Education (COE) that resides in the University of Hawai‘i system—10 campuses and system offices. Founded in 1907 under the Morrill Act as a land-grant college of agriculture and mechanical arts, the University of Hawai‘i at Mānoa (UHM) is the flagship campus of the University of Hawai‘i system. Nearly 20,000 students are enrolled in this research-extensive institution, taking courses in-person, through hybrid models, or fully distance delivery. The UHM campus awards bachelor's degrees in 99 fields of study, 87 masters' degree programs, and 57 doctoral and professional degrees (University of Hawai'i at Manoa, n.d.).

The Ed.D. in Professional Educational Practice began development in 2009 with a set of meetings between the College of Education and its community partners—the Hawai‘i Department of Education (HiDOE), the Hawai‘i Association of Independent Schools (HAIS), Punahou Schools, The Kamehameha Schools, and others. Much like the discussions described by Shulman and colleagues (2006) about issues related to the efficacy and utility of a Ph.D. in educational leadership, these thought partners deliberated preparing school and district leaders to solve some of the most pressing problems facing Hawai‘i's schools such as poor academic performance, violence on campus, teacher and administrator shortage, etc.

With the assistance of Dr. David Imig (then CPED's director) and Dr. Hunter McEwan (the program's first director), institutional stakeholders and community partners explored the tenets of the CPED program design as they constructed the foundations of UHM's Ed.D. program. In the fall of 2011, the first cohort of 30 students launched. UHM's Ed.D. in Professional Educational Practice seeks to prepare scholarly educational leaders who work collaboratively, apply research and theory, reflect critically and ethically, and utilize a broad range of interdisciplinary perspectives to recognize, create, advocate, implement, evaluate, and enhance spaces of social justice across Hawaiʻi and beyond. Such scholarly practitioners resolve critical, complex problems of practice impacting their schools by collaborating with stakeholders, conducting practical, practice-based research, and applying (or creating) theory (Perry, 2013). The Ed.D. is accredited by the Western Association of Schools and Colleges (WASC) and AAQEP. The program received provisional approval in 2010 from the UH Board of Regents and approval as an established program in 2019.

A characteristic of UHM's Ed.D. Program is the interplay between its two capstones: The Group Consultancy Project (GCP) and the Dissertation in Practice (DiP). Both represent what Shulman (2005) describes as signature pedagogies that "organize the fundamental ways in which future practitioners are educated for their new professions" (p. 52). Both these projects integrate CPED's foundational principles with the UHM and College of Education's program requirements to fulfill the program's mission:

> The College of Education Ed.D. program, as part of the University of Hawaii system, is committed to improving the social, economic and environmental wellbeing of current and future generations" and its vision: "We envision educational leaders who work collaboratively, apply research and theory, reflect critically and ethically, and utilize broad, interdisciplinary perspectives to recognize, create, advocate, implement, evaluate, and enhance spaces of social justice across Hawaiʻi and beyond. (University of Hawaiʻi Ed.D. Cohort V Program Description, 2022a, p. 2)

How has UHM's Ed.D. Transformed?

To say that navigating through the design, construction, evaluation, and continued refinement of this program has been smooth sailing would be false. The journey has been fraught with challenges. Through four program leadership changes, two Deans, the loss of funders, significant budgetary issues, disputes concerning its legitimacy as representative of doctoral rigor, and a reduction in applications, the Ed.D. in Professional Educational Practice at UHM has weathered much. Yet, it has consistently supported an average of 25 new educational leaders prepared to advocate for social justice.

The program has several procedural and philosophic principles that have allowed it to maintain a steady course of growth, excellence, and success. First, this Ed.D. has always collected, analyzed, and utilized stakeholder data to make programmatic decisions. These include program evaluation data (primarily student data), faculty reviews, and community member/client program reviews.

Second, although leadership has shifted four times since its inception in 2009, a core group of community leaders has remained advocates of this Ed.D. program. These vital partners are the instructional staff, consultancy project advisors and mentors, and dissertation committee members. Several sit on the program's advisory committee and many in this support network have affiliations with the program for 5 years or more. The network consists of current and former school principals, heads of schools, district and state school system administrators, community leaders, CEOs, employers, and other active and retired educational and business leaders. Each new program director has leaned on these critical thought partners to refine this Ed.D. continuously, and at times, advocate for additional support of it. With this network of over 50 practitioner-leaders, the ability of this program to maintain relevance to and appropriateness in serving the needs of Hawai'i's educational community would not occur.

Although there are numerous other factors that contribute to its success—too many to record in this chapter—without the dedication of the program's leadership and staff, the heavy lift that accompanies the continuous improvement of UHM's Ed.D. in Professional Educational Practice would not occur. Every prior director put forth a variety of innovative, creative ideas for this program and was willing to deliberate the merits of each. From its very creation, the program has depended on a core group of support staff—secretaries such as Marsha Ninomiya and Marilou Matuura—and graduate assistants like Veselina Lambrev, Amy Sojot, Yuko Ida, and Poli'ahu Dulay.

Together, they have worked through difficult system requirements, maintained open lines of communication between all stakeholders, and negotiated with others to keep the program operational. These individuals are the navigators and captains of this program and are some of the reasons why this Ed.D.'s voyage continues.

Creating the Group Consultancy Project

This program began with discussions concerning the value of doctorates in education. Concern echoed from practicing educational leaders about the applicability and relevance of a Ph.D. to educational practice. As Perry (2012) described, questions arose concerning time, energy, and funding commitments, as well as course content and processes associated with creating researchers and/or professors rather than practicing leaders. These community partners pushed for a more relevant, applicable doctorate.

To do so, the design team, along with CPED, developed the GCP that enables students to employ theory, literature, and research methods to address a critical problem of practice present in their school or district context. The design team drew inspiration from their professional experiences, a number of surveys sent to public school leaders, and contemporary research. Consultancies have been expansive and become contributions of this Ed.D. to the wider public. Since 2011, this Ed.D. has worked with 21 partner clients—P–12 schools, higher education campuses, community organizations, and public agencies—to produce 27 projects. These applied research studies are wide-ranging and conducted without financial costs to the client. The GCPs embody transformative learning experiences that apply community expertise to academic coursework and generate increased support for learners (Twomey & Lambrev, 2018).

Several issues arose with the first round GCPs. Some Cohort I members were asked to generate and pitch to their classmates their own projects, but because the projects were still under development, they lacked timeframes, clear definitions, scope and depth, and support resources such as structured advising/mentoring and negotiation with clients (University of Hawai'i Ed.D. Program Evaluation, 2014, 2016a). Four of six Cohort I consultancies took teams a year and a half to 2 years to complete, impacting the remaining time left in the 3.5 years of the program to complete their dissertation. A Cohort I student shared, "We had a hard time stopping the project. Had the project had more specifics and a deadline, we wouldn't have taken so long" (University of Hawai'i Ed.D. Program Evaluation, 2014, p. 12).

After the first cohort, the program and its stakeholders sought to improve the project's effectiveness, adopting a number of adaptations. The program set new parameters for project completion, began soliciting schools and educational organizations for project ideas, and recruited members from Cohort I to provide increased support to student teams. A project advisor sponsoring a Cohort II team stated:

> Because of the experiences of cohort I, we now understand the importance of the consultancy as a vehicle for applied learning and not as an end. The program needs to continue to put boundaries around it so that students and clients do not go beyond a year and a half to complete the project. (University of Hawai'i Ed.D. Faculty Review, 2016, p. 4)

One member of Cohort II described their consultancy experience, stating, "I appreciated that the program reviewed and assigned consultancy projects during the first summer, rather than waiting for the first fall semester" (University of Hawai'i Ed.D. Program Evaluation, 2016a, p. 2). A Cohort III student added, "I appreciate the limits placed on clients for asking too much. I thank our advisor and mentors for managing client expectations" (University of Hawai'i Ed.D. Program Evaluation, 2019a, p. 3). By the third cohort, the consultancy had evolved into a project "in which practitioner researchers take a functional approach to a problem of practice within a local community setting using an inquiry approach that privileges local knowledge in relationship with educational theory" (Twomey & Lambrev, 2018, p. 3).

Currently, this strategy continues to examine a problem of practice within a community educational setting using an inquiry approach that privileges local knowledge in conjunction with research, practice, and theory (University of Hawai'i Ed.D. Cohort V Program Description, 2022a). Community partners—participating agencies, schools, campuses, and organizations—submit requests for proposals (RFPs) presenting real problems that plague their educational practice in need of redress. These proposals must allow our learners to complete the project in a 6-month period, address a problem of practice that advances social justice (correct for injustices), incorporate forms of quality research methodologies, as well as integrate theoretical and research knowledge. Once the program reviews and approves proposals, the community partners present them to students. Thereafter, students rank their project preferences and the program faculty endeavor to match the students with their choices. A faculty advisor and a set of community mentors are also assigned to each GCP to guide the student teams and can assist with consultant–client negotiations to develop a clear, thoughtful project plan.

The program faculty also restructured the curriculum to align with what students need to produce a project for their clients successfully. Instead of teaching both quantitative and qualitative research methods in Year 2 of the program, students now receive instruction in both during the first year. Consultancies are now approximately 9 months in length, and several courses were redesigned to better support the progression of the teams. An initial course introduces the GCP process as students learn about the project guidelines and requirements, the RFPs, and the roles and responsibilities of members, community mentors, and project advisors. During the fall and spring terms of year one, consultancy-dedicated courses allow students to utilize knowledge gained from research courses to frame and refine their research question(s), their approach to data collection and analysis, and their approach for disseminating findings to the client and stakeholders. In these courses, students examine writing and organizational conventions, how to use continuous client feedback, and other strategies that ensure that the clients' needs are met adequately and appropriately.

In the last 4 years, the program has also developed the following resources for the consultancy strategy: a guidebook that defines and explains the process; a set of assessment rubrics for each phase of the project; workshops for project advisors and mentors about the project scope, data collection and analysis, reporting and presentation expectations; advisor and mentor discussions (approximately three times over the project period); and program evaluations—surveys, open-ended questionnaires, focus group protocols, and others.

Since the first year of our Ed.D. program, we have continually gathered data and monitored the progress of the project teams. These data came from clients, advisors, mentors, and students throughout the progression of the consultancies to ensure that the teams meet the needs of their clients. The program leaders offered advice and resources to teams when appropriate. Even students, advisors, mentors, and clients collaborate to determine the final grade for the projects.

The Group Consultancy Project remains a key strategy for the UHM Ed.D. program to support the preparation of educational leaders who are able to conduct research that is rigorous, ethical, and makes a positive difference in the lives of individuals, families, schools, and communities. In a survey conducted in 2016 with students, advisors, and mentors, Cohort II learners reportedly spent upwards of 80 hours within a 1- to 2-week period in client meetings and as much as 160 or more hours for at least a 4-week period working with their client, advisors, and mentors in completing their Consultancy Project (Ed.D. Program Evaluation, 2016a). A study (Twomey & Lambrev, 2018) conducted by a group of faculty, mentors, and students found that the consultancy remains a collaborative "inquiry-in-action" and demonstrates "a potential to transform students' and clients' practices by enhancing the cultural-discursive, material-economic, and social-political arrangements that shape the leadership practice in consultancy project partnerships" (Twomey & Lambrev, 2018, p. 15).

Transforming the Concept of Social Justice

In designing the first cohort, the program adopted the six CPED principles to describe what it hoped to develop in students over the course of the 3.5 years (Twomey & Lambrev, 2018). During a strategy session in 2014, stakeholders convened and refined the principles into four essential student learning objectives: 1) Work collaboratively to solve problems and implement plans of action; 2) Apply research to bring about improvements in problems of practice; 3) Reflect ethically and critically on matters of educational importance; 4) Take a broad interdisciplinary perspective on educational issues. Further development of student learning outcomes during the 2019–20 academic year conducted with a new stakeholder group produced six wisdoms:

1. *Praxis Wisdom*: application(s) and action(s) that resolve a problem of practice—an ethical, equity, and/or social justice issue impacting community—through *pono* (e.g., righteous, morally right, appropriate) ways.
2. *Academic Wisdom*: skills, knowledge, and disposition—writing, research, scholarship, time management, continual improvement, reflection, others—that allow for successful navigation of this doctorate program and other academic endeavors.
3. *Collective Wisdom*: the building and strengthening of relationships, receiving and sharing of knowledge, ideas, and thoughts, as well as other collaborative approaches that contribute to the betterment of all.
4. *Social Justice Wisdom*: appropriate forms of advocacy and action that result in the improvement of equality, equity, and forms of decision making that uphold and protect the rights, liberties and humanity of all.
5. *Innovation Wisdom*: new ways of thinking, exploring, creating, and working to produce new and better solutions.
6. *Spiritual/Inner Wisdom*: ways of being, knowing, believing, and valuing that promote peace, integrity, inspiration, compassion, sensitivity, reflection, resilience, and efficaciousness. (University of Hawai'i Ed.D. Cohort V Program Description, 2022a, p. 1)

Such iterations of student learning expectations reflect the program's commitment to its ongoing journey in search of improved learning and practice.

As a noted community mentor, Dr. Dan White reminded program stakeholders that since the program's inception, one of the most significant tasks has been to define and refine what social justice means in the context of education in the Hawai'ian Islands. Although roughly 50% of each cohort are Native Hawai'ian and Pacific Islander educators (AAQEP, 2021) and over 67% of all consultancy projects and capstones (dissertations-in-practice) topics have focused on issues of ethnicity, gender, culture, and other injustices, comments from students throughout the cohorts have continually attested to the ambiguity of what the program defines as social justice. "What is the utility of focusing on inequalities and injustice?" mentioned a Cohort I student (University of Hawai'i Ed.D. Program Evaluation, 2014, p. 3). "I still don't understand what social justice has to do with good teaching?" wrote a student from Cohort II while completing the consultancy project (University of Hawai'i Ed.D. Program Evaluation, 2016a, p. 5).

Within the span between the 2014 strategic planning meeting and the 2020 development of the wisdoms, program leaders, faculty, community advisors, and students grappled with determining not only what social justice looks like in Hawai'i (and the rest of the Pacific) but also how to actuate it in educational settings. At the 2019 CPED convening in Lincoln, Nebraska, the program directors participated in a session conducted by East Carolina University. The presentation highlighted the value of defining social justice and we retooled the program's commitment to its activation by describing student learner outcomes as wisdoms that students both processed and could *ho'o'ulu* (continue to grow). The draft of these wisdoms was then vetted with the advisory committee, faculty, community mentors, and students.

These wisdoms were adopted in 2020, and work groups consisting of faculty, community mentors, and students examined and created curricular and assessment recommendations. As a Cohort III member shared, "I would like to get exposed more to different frameworks, as well as methodologies: in-depth discussions/activities where we talk about readings/theories and how we would apply these to our practice and our research" (University of Hawai'i Ed.D. Program Evaluation, 2020a, p. 6). Since adopting these wisdoms (for Cohort IV), 22 of 26 cohort IV participants ranked high (9 or 10 on a 10-point scale) the program's ability to broaden their skills and knowledge to address a diverse set of educational issues, and 21 rated high (9 or 10 on a 10-point scale) the program's ability to engage them in the advancement of social justice (University of Hawai'i Ed.D. Program Evaluation, 2020a). In terms of curriculum, 23 of 26 rated the program high on its ability to promote ethical and critical reflection and interaction (University of Hawai'i Ed.D. Program Evaluation, 2021b). Although the results of the 2022 evaluations have yet to be fully analyzed, as one community mentor noted, "This program has undergone a lot of changes, especially on combatting social injustices at every level of this state's educational systems" (University of Hawai'i Ed.D. Program Evaluation, 2022b, p. 13).

Starting with Cohort IV, from the point of admission to graduation, cohort members, faculty, mentors, and consultancy clients provide data examining the *ho'oulu* of these wisdoms. Cohort IV students noted: "This class exposed me to new ideas centered around equity, colonization, and privilege. The weekly journal prompts while at times frustratingly challenging taught me to write and think about these topics" while another wrote, "When I think about social justice and equity . . . [the] class really was the epitome of what educational leaders should be learning about" (University of Hawai'i Ed.D. Program Evaluation, 2021b, p. 2). Yet, even as the program celebrates the progress made in refining what social justice means here in the islands, it must be acknowledged that the work continues. As one of the students put it, "I think when microaggressions (in a class) are conducted we must pause and elevate them . . . when issues occurred . . . it was handled poorly" (University of Hawai'i Ed.D. Program Evaluation, 2021b, p. 2).

Transforming the Dissertation-in Practice

Initial start-up discussions among program faculty to define the Dissertation in Practice (DiP) in UHM's Ed.D. Program in Professional Educational Practice yielded the following:

> an inquiry project with a focus on making an original contribution to practice rather than to knowledge. The project, conducted over four semesters of the program, is an opportunity for each member of the cohort to pursue work of personal professional interest. As the emphasis of the professional practice dissertation project is on seeking, in an informed way, solutions to problems of practice, the approach to be pursued is also different from traditional dissertation research work. Professional practice research problems arise in the professional experiences of practitioners and actively involve

> participant researchers in an investigation into their own practice. (Twomey & Lambrev, 2018, p. 6)

Currently, the first eight courses delivered in the first year are dedicated to the completion of the consultancy projects while the latter 40 credits, or 14 courses, support the completion of the dissertation. However, the voyage to get to this aligned curriculum, as previously stated, has been both stormy and at times, chaotic. Cohort I consultancy teams spent an average of 1.5 to 2 years on their projects, leaving 1.5 years to conduct and complete their dissertations. Six cohort members requested an extension to conclude their DiPs and of these, two did not finish. Cohort II had five extensions with all completing and Cohort III had ten delayed DiPs with two completed thus far. This Ed.D. continues to work toward completion of both capstones by all cohort members within the 3.5 program years.

Another aspect of the DiP under refinement is the shaping of practitioner-scholars. "The Ed.D. aims to build upon this authentic knowledge while challenging candidates to apply theory and research to address problems of practice within their educational context" (Twomey & Lambrev, 2018, p. 8). The DiP should support the growth of practitioner-scholars who integrate professional knowledge and expertise with theory, research, and literature to address a problem in their practice (Knapp, 2017).

Since adopting the six wisdoms as learning objectives and aligning the curriculum to address them, students have commented on the expedition. "I did not start as a scholar. I didn't get into the Ed.D. wanting to do research or necessarily understanding why I should. I get why now" (University of Hawai'i Ed.D. Program Evaluation, 2020a, p. 4). "Not too sure about this research and writing thing. I'm getting it now but I was lost at the beginning" (University of Hawai'i Ed.D. Program Evaluation, 2021b). "So far, I had to learn new knowledge, concepts and skills developed in the class longer than most students in the class. I had to reread the text, repeat exercises, and rewrite many reflections that I had to turn in" (University of Hawai'i Ed.D. Program Evaluation, 2020a, p. 4). We found, as have others (e.g., Rigler et al., 2021), that the shift from a more traditional doctoral scholar to one that promotes practitioner scholarship challenges university programs to rethink what constitutes rigor and preparation for the doctoral journey.

Writing support

Throughout the four cohorts, the program has instituted a number of strategies to support the completion of the dissertation. First, a more appropriate time to complete both capstones enables more students to generate quality products in a timely manner. Second, the program recognizes the need to better prepare participants for the individual research and writing necessary to accomplish a DiP. "I wish I learned how to write well. Even though I just completed my master's paper, when I got into this program, I quickly found myself struggling as a writer" (University of Hawai'i Ed.D. Program Evaluation, 2014, p. 8). "This student needs additional support to improve her writing capacity. Her grammar and sentence structure are patterned after ___ (non-English language) and seems to be affecting her ability to write coherently" (University of Hawai'i Ed.D. Program Evaluation, 2019a, pp. 8–9). "Overall, am enjoying the Ed.D. program; just don't feel very accomplished as a research writer" (University of Hawai'i Ed.D. Program Evaluation, 2021b, p. 10). To ensure support was available to students, the program instituted a writing workshop for Cohort II, two dedicated writing courses for Cohort III, and a writing course, writing retreat, and language patterning coaching (for a few speakers of Hawaiian) for Cohort IV. The program hopes to continue expanding writing support for upcoming cohorts. A fourth research class—a mixed methods course—was dropped and replaced with the above and a DiP course was reshaped to include an emphasis on writing.

Chair selection

Over the course of the four cohorts, the program realized that matching students with dissertation chairs, especially aligning students' topic of study with the expertise of the chair, is complex and required more thought. In Cohort I, students were assigned by the program to a dissertation chair and a community member. Currently, with the fourth cohort, matches between chairs and students are co-constructed. These conversations have led to more symmetry between doctoral candidates and professors as well as dissertation committee members (from the community). "I feel like my chair and my committee understand me and I them. I'm glad to have chosen them" and "I am learning so much from my committee" (University of Hawai'i Ed.D. Program Evaluation, 2021b, p. 6).

Modification of courses and experiences

As a part of this Ed.D.'s vision to "work collaboratively, apply research and theory, reflect critically and ethically, and utilize broad, interdisciplinary perspectives" (University of Hawai'i Ed.D. Cohort V Program Description, 2022a, p. 3), courses and programmatic experiences have been modified to reflect contemporary leadership problems of practice. The program often utilizes the practicing school and community leaders to co-teach with the college's faculty or individually. "I have learned a lot about the 'real' world of leadership from community partners" (University of Hawai'i Ed.D. Faculty Review 2016, p. 7). "They [Community Members] take a theory and translate it into something that the student understands how to use (University of Hawai'i Ed.D. Faculty Review, 2019, p. 6).

New and innovative frameworks

Finally, there have been concerted efforts over the last 11 years of existence to support new DiP formats, research frameworks, approaches and theory, and other ways to conduct these investigations. Instructors continue to utilize the traditional five-chapter format to engage students in developing DiP structures that are appropriate for their study and research agenda. In the case of Indigenous scholarship, several Native Hawaiians and Pacific Islanders in each cohort have generated formats that align with Indigenous principles and epistemologies. Even what constitutes research data has been examined through the dissertation process. Recently, one dissertation looked at stories produced through dreams—a culturally grounded and accepted form of knowledge for Native Hawaiians—as data for a dissertation that addressed how a person's cultural epistemologies and knowledge develop into pedagogical approaches for the benefit of kindergarten children (Reid-Hayes, 2020). This program continues to explore the horizons of research to develop new solutions to current and future problems of practice.

Change and Innovation

While change and transformation may be difficult if nearly impossible (Fischbacher et al., 2021; Gallagher et al., 2019), both are critical to producing innovative strategies and practices that advance education. Along the lines of what Rogers (2003) recognizes as innovative activities, this program has long utilized data gathered from multiple sources, the most important of which are the voices of students (Pape et al., 2022), to identify and prioritize problems of practice. The program continues to collaborate with practitioner leaders to enable its curricular approaches, assessments, and capstones to be relevant and meaningful. Just as these active collaborations designed the Consultancy capstone, the DiPs with community members on committees continue to address real, critical issues affecting education in the islands as well as test solutions that incorporate theory and research with practice. By blending academic research with professional expertise, solutions are tested through a process of trialability, and data are collected and analyzed to determine which solutions should be implemented over a larger span of time. This Ed.D. also has incorporated consistent and continued communication between partners and the program as well as scanned new developments shared by other Ed.D. programs to improve its relevancy.

Moreover, continuous improvement of this program is of utmost importance. Rogers (2003) noted five characteristics of change that appear throughout the life of this program. In terms of "relative advantage," the added writing support for students has increased and advanced. This Ed.D. initially began with writing workshops and by the second cohort, dedicated to the institutionalization of a writing course. Feedback from students and their dissertation advisors indicated that a single course did not meet the needs of a majority of the students. Two writing courses were offered for Cohort III; writing retreats and linguistic coaching were added for Cohort IV to address the needs of English-second-language learners. Linguistic coaching in particular supports these learners to understand, compare, and contrast language, grammar, and differences between languages to improve their capacity in the writing of their dissertation.

Data continue to be a cornerstone of this Ed.D. For the program to be able to adjust programming to advance students, each new innovation undergoes a process of design, testing, data collection, analysis, and discussion as a part of its continuous improvement. This process is what Rogers (2003) described as trialability, which is the degree to which an innovation can be experienced firsthand on a limited basis. "I'm not surprised that this Ed.D. looks too different from previous ones. It's clear that there were flaws in how things were done and something needed to change" (University of Hawai'i Ed.D. Program Faculty Review, 2020b, p. 12). "Although it consumes time and energy, the program directors always ask for input and evaluation of the program. They target specific aspects of the program to address . . . it's never dull or boring or meaningless. I feel like they are really interested in my feedback" (University of Hawai'i Ed.D. Program Faculty Review, 2022c, p. 12).

This ongoing commitment to include other sources of wisdom—folks from Carnegie Foundation's Improvement Science, community thought partners, faculty, current and past students—enable this Ed.D. to innovate and transform. Continuous improvement complements Rogers' change discussion in that preliminary solutions to problems are designed, implemented, and tested through short burst of innovations (Bryk et al., 2015). Such exploratory examinations also illuminate the complexity of each problem as well as the adjustments being made to solve them through a Plan-Do-Study-Act format (D'Amico et al., 2022).

Summary

The ongoing refinement of UHM COE's Ed.D. in professional practice has prepared it for a few exciting expeditions in the near future. Developed through multiple conversations with governments, thought partners, research agencies, funders, and former students, this new cohort intends to recruit teams of educational leaders from across the Pacific into what is being called the Pacifica Ed.D.

> To support native communities across the Pacific, the University of Hawai'i, College of Education's Doctorate in Professional Educational Practice is pursuing a mission to 'grow educational leaders who are committed to improving the social, educational, spiritual, economic, and environmental wellbeing of current and future generations'. Our program envisions 'educational leaders who work collaboratively, apply research and theory, reflect critically and ethically, and utilize broad, interdisciplinary perspectives to recognize, create, advocate, implement, evaluate, and enhance spaces of social justice across Hawai'i and beyond.' (University of Hawai'i Ed.D. Program Brochure, Pacifica Ed.D., 2021a)

Although currently undergoing curricular and system discussions, it is hoped that this new cohorted program will begin in 2025 with a group of 20 to 24 members.

In conversations with Hawai'i's Department of Education, we are also exploring the creation of a specialized K–12 public school leadership cohort that would house 10 to 15 current HiDOE leaders—school-level administrators as well as complex area and system leaders. In its initial stages of development, a team of former and current school leaders—more than half graduates of this program, faculty with expertise in K-12 leadership, grant funders, and others have coalesced to begin discussions. The need to increase the number of practitioner scholars in Hawai'i's public, K–12 schools continues to be an issue of concern emanating from multiple stakeholders.

The metaphor of the *wa'a*—wayfinding, seafaring, traditional navigation—is both archetypal and exemplary of this program's journey. We, the authors of this chapter, are both proud and honored to have sustained a commitment to continuously refine and enhance this program. We are also honored to be recognized by the AAQEP visiting team as one of the premiere programs in the college.

> Our case for Standard 3 indicates that the COE advanced programs have the capacity both internally and with partners to ensure that completers are prepared and succeed professionally. All of the advanced programs in the UHM COE offer a variety of clinical experience opportunities, but only one, the Ed.D. in Professional Practice, requires it for completion of the degree. (AAQEP Accreditation Report, 2021, p. 2)

The hope is that the program continues this long tradition as it expands its service to communities both here in the Hawaiian Islands and throughout the Pacific.

References

AAQEP. (2021). University of Hawai'i AAQEP Accreditation Report.

Bryk, A. S., Gomez, L. M., Grunow, A., & LeMahieu, P. G. (2015). *Learning to improve: How America's schools can get better at getting better*. Harvard Education Press.

D'Amico, L. K., West, H. S., Baker, M. A., Roy, G., Curcio, R., Harbour, K. E., ... & Adgerson, A. (2022). Using improvement science to implement and evaluate a teacher residency program in rural school districts. *Theory & Practice in Rural Education, 12*(1), 83–104. https://doi.org/10.3776/tpre.2022.v12n1p83-104

Fischbacher, C. M., Lewsey, J., Muirie, J., & McCartney, G. (2021). A critical reflection on the use of improvement science approaches in public health. *Scandinavian Journal of Public Health, 50*(3), 389–394. https://doi.org/10.1177/1403494821990245

Gallagher, H. A., Gong, A., Hough, H. J., Kennedy, K., Allbright, T., & Daramola, E. J. (2019). *Engaging district and school leaders in continuous improvement: Lessons from the 2nd year of implementing the CORE Improvement Community*. Policy Analysis for California Education, PACE. https://edpolicyinca.org/sites/default/files/CORE_Gallagher_Jan-2019.pdf

Knapp, M. S. (2017). The practice of designing qualitative research on educational leadership: Notes for emerging scholars and practitioner-scholars. *Journal of Research on Leadership Education, 12*(1), 26–50. https://doi.org/10.1177/1942775116647365

Pape, S. J., Bryant, C. L., JohnBull, R. M., & Karp, K. S. (2022). Improvement science as a frame for the dissertation in practice: The Johns Hopkins experience. *Impacting Education: Journal on Transforming Professional Practice, 7*(1), 59–66. https://doi.org/10.5195/ie.2022.241

Perry, J. A. (2012). To Ed. D. or not to Ed. D.? *Phi Delta Kappan, 94*(1), 41–44. https://doi.org/10.1177/003172171209400108

Perry, J. A. (2013). Carnegie Project on the Education Doctorate: The education doctorate—A degree for our time. *Planning and Changing, 44*(3/4), 113–126.

Reid-Hayes, D. E. K. (2020). *There is beauty in the space between child and teacher: A Moʻokūʻauhau of a Kanaka ʻŌiwi Early Childhood Educator (An ʻŌiwi Moʻolelo Research Study)* (Doctoral dissertation, University of Hawai'i at Manoa).

Rigler Jr., K. L., Anastasia, C. M., El-Amin, A., & Throne, R. (2021). Scholarly voice and academic identity: A systematic review of doctoral student agency. In K L. Rigler Jr., C. M. Anastasia, A. El-Amin, & R. Throne (Eds.), *Handbook of research on developing students' scholarly dispositions in higher education*, (pp. 63–89). IGI Global.

Rogers, E. M. (2003). *Diffusions of innovations* (5th ed.). The Free Press.

Shulman, L. S. (2005). Signature pedagogies in the professions. *Daedalus, 134*(3), 52–59.

Shulman, L. S., Golde, C. M., Bueschel, A. C., & Garbedian, K. J. (2006). Reclaiming education's doctorates: A critique and a proposal. *Educational Researcher, 35*(3), 25–32. https://doi.org/10.3102/0013189X035003025

Spiller, C., Barclay-Kerr, H., & Panoho, J. (2015). *Wayfinding leadership: Groundbreaking wisdom for developing leaders.* Huia Publishers.

Twomey, S. J., & Lambrev, V. (2018). University of Hawai'i at Mānoa, Ed.D. Program of the Year Application.

University of Hawai'i at Mānoa. (n.d.). About UH Mānoa. Retrieved February 23, 2023 from https://manoa.hawaii.edu/about/

University of Hawai'i Ed.D. (2022a). Cohort V Program Description.

University of Hawai'i Ed.D. (2021a). Program Brochure, Pacifica Ed.D.

University of Hawai'i Ed.D. (2014). Program Evaluation.

University of Hawai'i Ed.D. (2016a). Program Evaluation.

University of Hawai'i Ed.D. (2019a). Program Evaluation.

University of Hawai'i Ed.D. (2020a). Program Evaluation.

University of Hawai'i Ed.D. (2021b). Program Evaluation.

University of Hawai'i Ed.D. (2022b). Program Evaluation.

University of Hawai'i Ed.D. (2016b). Program Faculty Review.

University of Hawai'i Ed.D. (2019b). Program Faculty Review.

University of Hawai'i Ed.D. (2020b). Program Faculty Review.

University of Hawai'i Ed.D. (2022c). Program Faculty Review.

CHAPTER FIVE

Drexel University's Ed.D. in Leadership and Management—Ensuring Program Quality in the Face of High Enrollments

HARRIETTE THURBER RASMUSSEN
AND DEANNA HILL

It seemed like a good problem to have—too many students. As is often the case in complex environments, a problem solved can create new challenges—and expose aspects of a program that ultimately lead to new directions. This chapter is about new directions that came about through Drexel University's innovative response to a problem of practice, using its best thinking at the time. Much has happened between the conception of the innovation that won CPED's Program of the Year (POY) award in 2019 and our Ed.D. program today, which is still evolving and still suffering from "good" problems.

This chapter will examine that evolution and its impact on faculty, students, and the communities intended to benefit from Drexel's Ed.D. graduates through the lens of Rogers' (2003) diffusion of innovation theory. It will begin with an examination of Drexel's Ed.D. journey through Rogers' first two stages of innovation processes: agenda setting—recognition of a problem and matching an innovative solution. We will explain the origins of Drexel's POY award application, the collaborative efforts to address the award component, and the ways in which the program's communication channels and social systems came together to create an award-winning application. We will then move on to Rogers' third stage of innovation, redefining, in which not only the innovation itself but a number of foundational aspects of the program—noted in the POY application—were revisited based on numerous data sources and continued work with CPED's principles (CPED, n.d.). Rogers (2003) explains redefining as a component of implementation, where an innovation is modified or adjusted as it is implemented. Due perhaps to Drexel's collaborative and diffusing culture, ongoing implementation of its POY award-winning innovation led to a reexamination of some of the theories and practices upon which the program had been founded—and which were outlined in our POY application. The clarifying processes (Rogers' fourth stage) have resulted in some significant design adjustments that extend beyond the boundaries of the award but were set in motion through the POY application process. In other words, the processes of innovation continue. This chapter will end with a reflective coda, considering the ways in which the award process ultimately led to a continuous process of programmatic self-reflection and adaptation.

Agenda Setting: Capitalization on Good Problems

Drexel's POY application began by outlining several defining features of the School of Education in which its Ed.D. program is housed: "A comprehensive, civically-engaged, practice-oriented school in a private, nonprofit R1 university that places high-quality, experiential teaching and learning at the center of everything we do" (Drexel University CPED POY Application, 2019, p. 5). This context is critical to understanding the choices made to (1) orient the Ed.D. program to transformative learning (Mezirow, 1991), (2) incorporate aspects of experiential learning (Kolb, 2015), (3) spiral and scaffold the program elements (Bruner, 1960), (4) integrate concepts of mastery learning into coursework (Wiggins & McTighe, 2011), and (5) incorporate equity and decolonization perspectives into coursework and research pursuits (Patel, 2015; Smith 2012). Our application explained how the curriculum's scaffolded design drew upon concepts from systems and design thinking in the process of framing a constructivist approach to leadership, research, and sense-making. Students are exposed to adaptive leadership (Heifetz & Linsky, 2017) and the ways in which complex problems require different ways of leading. They explore the origins of their own framing of practitioner problems of practice through Senge's (1990) Iceberg Model. They explore empathic listening through Scharmer's (2016) Theory U and are introduced to prototyping and design thinking (Brown, 2008; Scharmer, 2016). Importantly, students explore these key concepts through the program's emphasis on equity and social justice, completing their leadership series with an examination of critical epistemologies and establishing an important framing for how students consider themselves to be social justice leaders.

The result of our approach to the Ed.D. degree was startling growth, growing from 60 to 300 students in a decade. Our application in 2019 noted that "in that year, we enrolled nearly as many students as we had graduated in the past ten years" (Drexel University CPED POY Application, 2019, p. 12). Our *good problem* required innovative responses to ensure that the quality of our program remained constant for the larger number of students we now served. The act of *agenda setting* led to what Rogers (2003) terms a *matching* process—figuring out how to solve the problem through innovation. We focused attention on our mentoring and advising systems, using technology and forums to enhance our student support systems, all of which mapped to CPED design concepts (CPED, n.d., Mentoring and Advising Design Concept). Students access self-paced courses in the *Publication Manual of the American Psychological Association* (APA) 7 rules, library research, mindfulness, etc., at orientation in order to front-load some of the key skills they will draw upon during their life as doctoral students. Our first-year courses focused on foundational leadership and research classes, with careful scaffolding and iterative writing that ultimately led to students' dissertation proposals. As stated in our POY application, our goal was to engage students in "an evolutionary writing process through assignments that bridge courses to support a dynamic iterative and recursive conceptual design" (Drexel University CPED POY Application, 2019, p. 13). Students began concentration courses in their second year, along with a series of research methods courses with a pilot study to gain experience collecting, analyzing, and communicating data, results, and recommendations. By the time students started working with a dissertation supervising professor, they had significant exposure to research proposal components, our dissertation handbook, and extensive feedback from a variety of professors, intended to (1) expand their perspectives on research design, (2) develop their writing capacity, and (3) position them to finalize and defend their research proposal in their 9th quarter of study.

The program's design intended to allow our cohort-based communities of learners to draw upon each other and the scaffolded curriculum. The award application noted how we increased student access to the program manager and advising team, taking into account the fact that our students, full-time working professionals, are promised a fully online program. We added multiple connection points for students, including a cross-cohort Open Advising Hour each quarter to "share information informally and provide an open forum for students to engage, question, and provide feedback to the program" (Drexel University CPED POY Application, 2019, p. 16). As our application explained, the Open Advising Hour "was a critical advancement . . . as it provided a safe space at a flexible time in the evening . . . conducive to dynamic learning, open communication, and peer-to-peer support" (Drexel University CPED POY Application, 2019, p. 16). At these forums, students could connect with students from other cohorts, meet faculty members, see members of the advising team, and position themselves in the midst of a greater learning community dedicated to their success.

New faculty role

These structures and systems intending to support the scholarly practitioner did not entirely solve the problem of rapid enrollment growth and concerns about faculty capacity. The number of students needing supervising professors for their research outpaced our institutional capacity, so we created a new clinical faculty position primarily responsible for supervising dissertations, with some teaching and service obligations. A key feature of our POY application, the position was piloted in 2016 as "an opportunity for faculty to focus specifically on dissertation advising as a practice" (Drexel University POY Application, 2019, p. 23) and to develop multiple systems to work with multiple students in the same phase of their dissertation research. Our POY application described one such system to enhance our students' sense of belonging to a community of learners called the Doc Student Support Group. Modeled after the Critical Friends Group process developed by the Annenberg Institute for School Reform at Brown University, the voluntary Zoom-based bi-monthly sessions intended to provide a "safe intellectual space for students to muse over issues and concerns" (Drexel University POY Application, 2019, p. 18) and receive feedback from their supervising professor and peer group. While Drexel's courses routinely incorporate peer feedback, these conversations are faculty-guided, pushing students to think more deeply and critically about their and others' work but in a collaborative setting so that students can learn from others' experiences. Students reported a "self-imposed accountability mechanism" (Drexel University POY Application, 2019, p. 18) and that they looked forward to these sessions.

The Best Laid Plans . . .

Diffusion of innovation theory accounts for adjustments to an innovation that occur through the diffusion process. Termed redefining and restructuring, Rogers (2003) posits that this stage "occurs when the innovation is re-invented so as to accommodate the organization's needs and structure more closely, and when the organization's structure is modified to fit with the innovation" (p. 424). These advising approaches, a new faculty role, peer support groups, etc., were examples of Rogers' redefining and restructuring phases of the diffusion of innovations (DOI) and came about through collaborative mechanisms that allowed for feedback and organizational learning. Researchers (e.g., Tyre & Orlikowski, 1994) note that these modifications need to take place before the new structure becomes firmly embedded into the innovating organization, and Drexel's structures continued to evolve due to what Rogers terms *clarifying*. In the DOI model, clarifying represents widespread implementation as a "new idea gradually becomes clearer" (Rogers, 2003, p. 427) to those involved. In our case, clarifying often moved us back to redefining and restructuring, representing a continuing evolution as opposed to a more linear process. One explanation might be that the nature of these innovations involved so many stakeholders: faculty, advising staff, and students—and the intentional dialogue that was at the heart of their implementation. Recall, for example, that the Open Advising Hour intended to get feedback from students on their experiences that covered multiple cohorts across multiple years. Dialogue also takes place through an Ed.D. Advisory Council (EAC) that meets monthly to advise the program director. The EAC consists of Ed.D.-dedicated faculty plus representatives from other departments, including those that house Drexel's concentration courses, such as nurse education and/or educational administration. Furthermore, Drexel's School of Education (SoE) enjoys a collaborative culture. Its monthly faculty meetings embrace discourse and feedback as to programmatic challenges. Because all SoE faculty supervise Ed.D. dissertations, student successes and challenges are regularly noted. So one might say that the actual diffusion process of the innovation that won the POY award in 2019 led to some rethinking, as well as expanding the basic structures upon which the program is based.

Exploring the student experience

As noted above, faculty input, EAC members, and advising staff now had a direct pipeline to the Ed.D. program director. The Ed.D. program director began to note persistent patterns across conversations and gathered formal data about student trends, reported challenges, and opportunities to refine the program further. The Ed.D. program director put together a cross-role data team that included advising staff, program administration, a Ph.D. student, and faculty to examine student experiences systematically and in greater depth, including those who left the program before completion or went on extended leaves of absence. Surveys, focus groups, retreats, and continued conversation led to some conclusions about the program design. We learned that many of the structures and systems described in our POY application had been successful. The emphasis on belonging and learning communities through the cohort model had its desired effect. Students said they felt valued by the faculty and connected to the program. The close student-to-student relationships developed through the cohort model were experienced by most students. The diversity of student backgrounds and perspectives enhanced students' learning as they were able to see course content through new lenses. We also confirmed what many of us had noticed through teaching and advising patterns that had led to the initiation of the data team. Some of the challenges suggested flaws in our original program design.

Iterative writing

Faculty had noted that the iterative design of proposal writing sometimes resulted in premature student commitment to research designs that were not fully informed. In other words, students began writing proposals before they were ready to develop a solid design, yet were often reluctant to revisit or discard earlier work. The original intent to scaffold the process with increasing layers of new knowledge related to the research process became a source of frustration for some students and for their eventual supervising professors who needed to redirect proposals. Students were also predisposed to qualitative studies, perhaps because the qualitative methods class was more extensive or because it was introduced before they studied quantitative methods. Other students felt unready to settle on a problem of practice so early in the program, wanting to explore a variety of topics, but then felt disadvantaged when they were asked to refine an earlier draft of a proposal that had been built around a problem of practice that was no longer—or had never been—compelling. Redirecting proposals from coursework resulted in proposal defenses later than had been promised, threatening the ability of students to complete the program within the 3-year design. Completion delays caused financial hardships for many of our students. By the time most students began working with their supervising professors exclusively, their coursework had required them to revise an initial research proposal multiple times. Finding out when they reached the proposal phase that there was more, sometimes significantly more, work to be done was an unhappy surprise. The challenges noted in our original POY award application, that "students often report negative feelings, such as guilt, shame, and frustration, related to their lack of progress" (Drexel University POY Application, 2019, p. 17), had not abated through our initial innovation.

Leadership and Concentration Courses

We also uncovered some challenges in the way we sequenced our leadership and concentration courses. Drexel's Ed.D. on leadership and management offers 11 concentrations. The intent of the program had been for the concentration content to stand on its own. However, students reported that leadership, concentration, and research learning were disconnected and felt that, in some concentrations, a deliberate link between concentration content and leadership courses would be advantageous. Running the leadership courses (in year one) prior to the concentration courses (year two) did not allow for intentional integration.

Charting progress

Drexel operated with a comprehensive exam system, outlined in its POY proposal as not only a benchmark assessment for students but also an opportunity for faculty to "engage in calibration" as they "scored the exams" (Drexel University POY Application, 2019, p. 9). The process of reviewing the exams enabled faculty to gain added exposure to curricular goals that were perhaps outside of their areas of specialization, e.g., Theory U, systems thinking, etc. And yet, even with a "comprehensive exam community" available to students for several months prior to taking the exam, our data showed high levels of anxiety and stress leading up to the exam. Too, charting the program's outcomes, or as they are referenced at Drexel, keystones, was a source of confusion for students as they did not always appear directly connected to coursework; the connections were explicit to faculty but not necessarily to students.

A New Generation of Diffusion

These challenges emerged during and following the POY award application process, which led to a new round of agenda-setting (Rogers, 2003) and to several years of dialogue with multiple stakeholders, including and especially students. Because of award-specific and CPED-aligned commitments, Drexel staff entered a phase that encompassed multiple DOI stages: matching for those areas that clearly needed a different approach, redefining areas that needed modification, and clarifying as we began to tweak innovations we were confident needed to continue. To be clear, the word innovation in this context is specific to Drexel and adjusting our own structures and systems. The story here is how diffusing our innovations led to new insights, causing us to recycle through the DOI phases before attempting routinization as a final phase. Most of us would agree that the field of higher education is shifting so rapidly that routinization, as Rogers may have envisioned, is, perhaps, no longer a goal, particularly in a world that suggests the need for continuous examination, reflection, and refining (or redirecting). Our program administrators and faculty made a number of adjustments in response.

Reconceptualizing iterative writing

We remain committed to the need for iterative writing. In many ways, we have strengthened the expectations that students rethink and revise their ideas and their writing. One example relates to our course in academic writing, in which students are now required to revise their work multiple times in response to various forms of feedback (peer, instructor, AI-generated) and provide evidence of the revisions. However, we also took a careful look at our course sequencing and aspects that caused students to prematurely fixate on a flawed research proposal and/or struggle to complete the proposal phase within the expected time frame.

The majority of our students intend to complete the program in 3 years and take two courses each term, one in the leadership/concentration track and a second in the research track. Students now begin their research track with our academic writing course, in which they thoroughly research the problem of practice they submitted in their application to the program. We tell them that while they may be an expert in that particular problem, their task is to now explore who else thinks this is a problem—and why—and the system in which the problem is situated. Their search for relevant literature emphasizes high-quality sources, teaches them how to do library research, and results in an argumentative literature review, emphasizing their practitioner perspective in conversation with the current literature. We place their work on our Ed.D. developmental writing rubric that explains a 2-year trajectory of academic writing skills across six modules. A key component of our Signature Assessment System (explained below) is that students are able to track their development in academic writing and seek additional support where needed.

From this class, they progress to an introductory overview course on research, followed by methods courses in quantitative and then qualitative research, before moving into a seminar course at the beginning of their second year. The seminar course, which we term a step-back opportunity, provides students the opportunity to consider their own research goals as they complete an exhaustive literature review that will frame their research proposal. At this point in time, they are assigned a supervising professor and have opportunities for an elective course, including options to hone their skills in a particular method. They then proceed to proposal writing in their final three terms of coursework, with 30 weeks to draft a proposal in close consultation with their supervising professor.

Emphasis on developing leaders

Relatedly, we have intentionally reduced the academic writing demands of our leadership courses to build more experiential components and relate what they are learning about leadership to the contexts of their concentration interests. While the essential content of these courses has not changed, i.e., systems and complexity, adaptive leadership, Theory U, etc., rather than teaching our students *about* leadership, we now emphasize developing them *as* leaders in ways that include non-written forms of communication, such as group dynamics and critical reflective practice. We have incorporated global leadership goals into our program outcomes that tightly align with our consistent approach to leadership that emphasizes personal awareness and development. Developed by global research teams of leadership and adult development experts to support the United Nations' global 2030 Sustainable Development Goals (United Nations, n.d.), these goals emphasize transformational skills in the areas of internal awareness *(Being: Relationship to Self)*, application of content knowledge and research skills *(Thinking: Cognitive Skills)*, empathic social-justice orientation *(Relating: Caring for Others and the World)*, capacity to learn with and from others *(Collaborating: Social Skills)*, and the ability plan and take strategic action *(Acting: Enabling Change)*.[1]

Developmental assessment

In the spring of 2020, the timing of our comprehensive exams coincided with the early lockdown days of the COVID-19 pandemic. Our students were already under extraordinary stress; adding an event we knew to be anxiety-provoking felt ill-advised. We had already begun to review the role of our comprehensive exams in predicting student readiness for the dissertation phase. The pandemic thus prompted a new agenda-setting and matching cycle to consider how ongoing assessments built into our course structure might be a more reliable indicator of student learning than a single high-stakes exam. The new Signature Assessment System was piloted in the Spring of 2020 in a single course taught to multiple sections of students. A common rubric was developed to measure critical course outcomes in that course (qualitative research), and the three faculty members teaching the course engaged in several rounds of moderation, calibrating samples of student work to the rubric to agree on expectations of quality. Our theory of action was twofold: that a common rubric would result in more consistent student development in key areas (in this case, research) and that explicit feedback would help our students and the faculty responsible for teaching them to better understand the specific areas that needed additional support.

Over the next year, the signature assessment system grew to encompass the students' entire span of coursework, assessing skill levels and progress in academic writing, oral communication, and research skills. Students are now placed on course-relevant rubrics six times across the first 2 years of the program, with the final rubric assessing a complete draft of their research proposal. The process of expanding the initial pilot required significant redefining and restructuring (Rogers, 2003). As faculty engaged with the rubrics, the instruments were adjusted to better reflect faculty expectations of students by clarifying language and the standards to which students would be held. Certain early aspects of the design were discontinued, such as a reflective component, in part because the speed at which we initiated the new system meant that some aspects of the design were simply not practical. Our attempts to clarify and routinize (Rogers, 2003) the signature system illustrated that our theory of action had been dependent upon systems that were not yet in place, such as a learning management system with the capacity to track student progress across multiple years. We also lacked the internal capacity to developmentally support student skill development as much as we had hoped. While we get these systems in place, the adjustments to the sequencing of our courses afford us the opportunity to sit comfortably in the clarifying phase as we determine how to best document and support student progress. Our original rubrics have been adjusted to the new course sequence, and a fourth developmental rubric now measures our revised leadership development goals. In some ways, our journey from comprehensive exams to a signature assessment system spans most of Rogers (2003) phases of innovation: from agenda setting to routinizing, while also illustrating the iterative nature of DOI itself.

Expanded Communities of Learners

We classify several of the innovations detailed in our POY application as routinized, the DOI stage where innovations achieve institutional normalcy, meaning they are no longer seen as novel. Our quarterly advising hours are firmly established as an opportunity for administrative and advising staff to check in with students and for cross-cohort collaboration. Another routinized innovation is our special faculty role to primarily supervise dissertations. There are now five full-time faculty members in this role. Faculty report on the rich learning and rewarding relationships this position holds—shepherding this final phase of so many different students, problems of practice, and methodologies with a clear lens for how to better prepare students for their contributions to research and practice.

The Doc Student Support Group has continued to evolve, with more students in varied phases of their research finding ways to help each other complete their degrees through structured protocols and the psychological safety brought by these mechanisms. While not quite routinized beyond specific faculty and their advisees, these support groups represent a continued quest to build the capacity of our student practitioners as scholars. We have also routinized virtual writing retreats, a practice that offers dedicated time for writing in the company of student "colleagues who care" with the opportunity for faculty consultations where needed. Held bi-monthly on Sunday afternoons, students commit to writing goals at the beginning of the session and report on their progress as they "check out" at the end. Students frequently note how productive these communal writing sessions are and how much they appreciate the collegiality at a time when, post-coursework, they often feel isolated. Faculty in attendance work on their own writing projects, modeling a continued commitment to writing and publishing.

We have also initiated several new innovations to support our community-of-learners orientation to the program. We have begun to explore the potential of team teaching in ways that bring students from other cohorts together for synchronous teaching sessions. Team teaching in this way has the added benefit of modeling peer learning to students while providing the additional perspective during class discussions available with the presence of additional faculty "in the room." Faculty have noted, too, that these joint sessions have expanded their own teaching practices and enhanced their confidence in navigating new ways of facilitating content. In other words, we, as faculty, get what we expect students to derive from the diversity in their group work: new perspectives and additional expertise. Team teaching has been routinized across several courses, and we expect the diffusion process will expand the practice.

MAC and DAC

Our mentoring programs have also become routinized, although expanded, building on the successes found through added opportunities for student and faculty interaction. Newer initiatives involve alumni in two ways: (1) through an Ed.D. Mentoring and Coaching Program (MAC) for first-year students and (2) as Dissertation Accountability Coaches (DAC) to support students in the dissertation phase. These innovations expand our community of learners to engage alumni who wish to give back to the program and its future alumni more intentionally. MAC offers guidance during that challenging first year on navigating doctoral studies through encouragement, resources, accountability, and, ultimately, building students' confidence. DAC intends to support students during that critical final phase of dissertation research in much the same way—as that external and committed cheerleader while providing an extra layer of support to ensure student success. In addition, we now have an Alumni Advisory Board, whose members serve as Alumni Ambassadors to support recruitment efforts and help prospective students determine if this program is the best fit for them. These examples help to explain the power of diffusion, as alumni play an increasing role in the Ed.D. program—because they want to. They gain new colleagues and networking opportunities while continuing their association with a cherished institution in a meaningful way.

Coda: Evolving Innovation

This chapter began with a discussion that framed the cornerstones of Drexel's Ed.D. program: transformative learning (Mezirow, 1991), experiential learning (Kolb, 2015), scaffolded and spiral learning (Bruner, 1960), mastery learning (Wiggins & McTighe, 2011), and equity and decolonization (Patel, 2015; Smith 2012), detailed in Drexel's program of the year application. These foundations still frame the program and provide a critical backdrop to all programmatic decisions as we continue to address persistent and new challenges. Our commitment to transformative leadership has evolved from a theoretical scholarly perspective to an experiential application as we strive to develop our students as leaders, not just teach them what others have learned and accomplished. We have refined our practice of experiential learning, adding the sometimes painful reflection and practice of leadership's toughest challenges to our pedagogy. Students learn about social justice and equity in real time as they deeply investigate how they affect others and act upon their values. Our practices around equity now include a more student-centered approach to assessment that maps skill and conceptual milestones with a focus on developmental interventions to support student success. We have expanded our practice in scaffolded and spiraled learning through an opportunity to integrate high-interest contexts (e.g., students' chosen concentrations) into leadership practices with our revised course sequence. We have also adjusted our research course sequencing to better meet students' learning needs, ease unnecessary frustration points, and support completion within the expected 3-year program trajectory. We have exposed and considered additional pathways to old and new challenges through the DOI process; one might say that we are where we are today because of the ways in which our POY innovations were diffused.

But as this chapter has demonstrated, innovations evolve. We are not done. Chosen strategies are, and always will be, best guesses, even when based on solid research and successes elsewhere. Theories of action are exactly that—theories to be tested, adapted, and tested again until confirmed—and only then until new conditions suggest further adaptation. Thus, we would argue that any and all innovations, by their very nature, intend to evolve and that it is through the process of diffusion that we understand the direction of that next innovation.

Until then . . .

Endnote

1. The italics represent the language of official Inner Development Goals (n.d.) and utilized by Drexel University's EdD program.

References

Brown, T. (2008). Design thinking. *Harvard Business Review, 86*, 84–92. www.hbr.org

Bruner, J. (1960). *The process of education*. Harvard University Press.

CPED (n.d.). The framework. https://www.cpedinitiative.org/page/framework

Drexel University. (2019). Drexel University POY Application.

Heifetz, R. A., & Linsky, M. (2017). *Leadership on the line: Staying alive through the dangers of leading*. Harvard Business Review Press.

Kolb, D. A. (2015). *Experiential learning: Experience as the source of learning and development*. Pearson Education.

Mezirow, J. (1991). *Transformative dimensions of adult learning*. Jossey-Bass.

Patel, L. (2015). *Decolonizing educational research*. Routledge.

Rogers, E. M. (2003). *Diffusion of innovations. Fifth edition*. Free Press.

Scharmer, O. (2016). *Theory U: Leading from the future as it emerges.* Berrett-Koehler Publishers.

Senge, P.M. (1990). *The fifth discipline.* Doubleday/Currency.

Smith, L. T. (2012). *Decolonizing methodologies: Research and indigenous peoples.* Zed Books.

Tyre, M. J., & Orlikowski, W. J. (1994). Windows of opportunity: Temporal patterns of technological adaptation in organizations. *Organizational Science 5*(1), 98–118.

United Nations. (n.d.). Sustainable Development Goals. https://www.undp.org/sustainable-development-goals

Wiggins, G., & McTighe, J. (2012). *Understanding by design. Guide to advanced concepts in creating and reviewing units.* Alexandria, VA: Association for Supervision and Curriculum Development.

CHAPTER SIX

Shaping, Scaffolding, and Structuring Practitioner Scholars' Research Preparation: An Inside-Out, Justice-Oriented Programmatic Innovation at the University of Florida

ALYSON ADAMS, NANCY FICHTMAN DANA, AND GAGE JETER

Faculty and students in the University of Florida's Teachers, Schools, and Society (TSS) Ed.D. program critically examine the dynamic interactions between the inner workings of educational institutions. The inner workings include the beliefs, values, and practices of educators and students, the distinctive features of curricula and pedagogy, and the initial and ongoing development of teachers and teacher educators and their larger societal contexts. Our consideration of these multi-faceted dimensions of education yields both nuanced and holistic portraits that inform our enduring and active commitment to vibrant and equitable schools for a healthy democracy.

Specifically, our Ed.D. program reinvents doctoral-level education as innovative job-embedded professional learning for working educators to support leaders, change agents, and advocates for all members of educational communities. Dedicated to collaboration with others to solve critical educational problems and to support educational professionals in diverse contexts with diverse learners, our Ed.D. program has a strong commitment to the CPED framework, as we have designed and enacted our program around "questions of equity, ethics, and social justice to bring about solutions to complex problems of practice" (CPED, n.d., Guiding Principle #1). Through inquiry-based recursive learning experiences (CPED, n.d., Guiding Principle #5), our primary program outcome is to prepare students to identify, examine, and redress inequities in diverse educational settings. Our students are practitioner-scholars, defined as "professionals who bring theoretical, pedagogical, and research expertise to bear on identifying, framing, and studying problems of practice and leading informed change in their schools and districts to continually improve life and learning conditions for students and adults who work within their local contexts" (Adams et al., 2014, p. 366).

To actualize this commitment, cohorts of students navigate three phases of our program that align with traditional Ph.D. program design but are conceptualized and enacted quite differently within our Ed.D. program: (1) coursework, (2) qualifying exams, and (3) dissertation. Intentionally scaffolded and sequenced, all courses similarly connect theory and research to practice and provide opportunities for students to think, question, and act. Though our program is primarily online, students engage in both asynchronous and synchronous learning experiences. The structure of our program enables students to work full-time anywhere in the world and use their work settings as laboratories of practice (CPED, n.d., Guiding Principle #4). *Try-it* strategies invite students to apply and assess concepts, theories, and research-informed practices in their local contexts. Coursework occurs during the first 2 years of the program and leads to qualifying exams. Upon successfully defending qualifying exams, students become doctoral candidates and enter our program's final phase: the Dissertation in Practice (DiP), a research experience focused on naming, framing, and studying a complex problem of practice to enact change in students' local contexts.

Given CPED guidelines and the literature emerging from Ed.D. programs, we adopted a DiP framework that honors the purposes of the professional practice doctorate, one of which is generating and transforming knowledge for, of, and in practice (CPED, n.d., Guiding Principle #6). Doctoral candidates develop a three-chapter product. In Chapter 1, students define a local problem of practice, use literature to suggest what might be done about it, and explain how they will study it. In Chapter 2, students describe what they have learned. In Chapter 3, students propose an action plan for themselves and others based on what they have learned in order to answer Auerbach's (2011) question, "How [will you] change your corner of the world?" (p. 69).

In accordance with our signature pedagogy, students move strategically through all aspects of the program together as a cohort that functions as a community of practice (Lave & Wenger, 1991). For three consecutive summers, students come to campus for a 1-week institute to engage collaboratively in critical conversations that cut across online course experiences and foster personal and professional relationships within and beyond the cohort essential to their developing identity as practitioner-scholars who work in and partner with diverse communities (CPED, n.d., Guiding Principle #3). Throughout our program, we use discussion protocols to structure both online (asynchronous and synchronous) and face-to-face communication. These protocols provide a series of steps that lead groups through intentional conversations that allow room for all participants' voices to be heard (e.g., McDonald et al., 2013). As students transition from coursework to qualifying exams, they divide into small research groups facilitated by faculty members who serve as mentors, advisors, and doctoral committee members; these group members support one another in the design and implementation of their action-oriented DiPs.

We achieved this intricate intertwining of CPED guiding principles and design concepts with our program's mission and content through our commitment to consistent collaboration and systematic, intentional learning from our own and our students' experiences in our program. One of our biggest challenges to date has been—and continues to be—enacting appropriate equity-focused research preparation for scholarly practitioners. The enduring dilemma of shaping, scaffolding, and structuring practitioner-scholars' research preparation is one shared by many CPED member institutions. For us, trying to reinvent Ed.D. research preparation within a university where the Ph.D. reigned supreme exacerbated the problem.

Origin and Journey

The University of Florida's status as a preeminent research-intensive institution posed challenges to adequately aligning with CPED's definition of the Ed.D. In particular, much as Andrews and Grogan (2005) asserted, the Ph.D. program format proved a hindrance (which they term a straitjacket) to our efforts to provide practitioners with the knowledge, skills, and dispositions needed to lead effectively in educational settings. Specifically, in the case of appropriate research preparation for practitioner-scholars, policies mandating the number and content of required doctoral research courses stymied our progress. Our students were required to take research methods courses that privileged quantitative approaches and the generation (rather than application) of theory, and viewed research embedded in one's context as inherently problematic. The immediate challenge facing us was that our respected, knowledgeable colleagues did not develop their research courses with the practitioner-scholar in mind.

What our students needed (and were not getting):

- Skills in how to conduct short cycles of improvement in their own context to quickly identify, investigate, evaluate, and revise practices;
- Instructors with an understanding of the educational contexts and roles of our students and the understanding that these contexts and roles are often shifting at lightning speed;
- Research processes and products conceptualized through a lens of equity and social justice;
- The knowledge and skills to read, understand, evaluate, and then communicate findings from research studies to stakeholders in their educational contexts; and
- An appreciation for knowledge-of-practice (Cochran-Smith & Lytle, 1993) where formal knowledge accompanies practical knowledge to problematize and improve classroom contexts through inquiry.

What they were getting (and did not need):

- Traditional research preparation, with a heavy emphasis on quantitative methods typically requiring large N studies and SPSS software;
- Research readings that privileged traditional university-based researchers as the producers of knowledge and theory; and
- Skills in how to conduct a thoughtful, carefully planned study that requires about a year to plan and conduct, but does not fit within a typical school calendar or realities of school contexts.

Thus began our ongoing journey to innovate traditional research preparation within a research-intensive university to meet the unique needs of scholarly practitioners.

Defining "Innovation"

This journey helped us understand that change from the outside-in can only progress so far, and what is needed is innovative change from the inside-out. Therefore, we define innovation not as a one-time event, but as a process of continually designing and redesigning our program from the inside-out rather than the outside-in. Inside-out program (re)design denotes our commitment to CPED guiding principles throughout our program, resulting in a cohesive and coordinated laser-like focus on the development of justice-oriented scholarly practitioners. In contrast, outside-in program (re)design imposes CPED principles and concepts into pre-existing Ph.D. doctoral preparation traditions, resulting in a sporadic and fragmented scholarly practitioner focus (i.e., a program where all CPED principles and concepts may be present, but not systematically and intentionally woven throughout the fabric of every program experience).

We came to our definition of innovation over time, as we learned from our experiences through conceptualizing the ongoing development and refinement of our decade-old Ed.D. program as a design-based research effort (Wang & Hannafin, 2005). With the goal of improving practice, design-based research has the following characteristics: pragmatic, grounded, interactive, flexible, integrative, and contextual (p. 7). As such, it shares qualities of practitioner scholarship and values of our signature pedagogy we hope to cultivate among our students.

As we examined our work on these issues through the lens of Rogers' (2003) Diffusion of Innovation, we were racing to *implement* our ideas, but we seemed stuck at the *initiation* stage in our college. While we had internal agreement within our TSS program on the *agenda-setting* stage, we lacked agreement within our college at the *matching stage*.

Innovative Processes and Phases

For our research methodology colleagues accustomed to teaching research courses face-to-face for Ph.D. students, preparing online courses for practitioner-scholars was a tall order. Having had 5 years of experience with an award-winning online master's program[1] for practitioners in Teacher Leadership for School Improvement, we were eager to share sample syllabi and weekly plans in our course shells, and to share what we had learned about powerful online instruction and course design. Although we facilitated some discussion of the purpose of the Ed.D. and the nature of the students who were admitted to our first cohort, our colleagues turned their attention to the shift from traditional to online instruction, keeping their course content relatively stable. That is, the mechanics of course design in the online environment took precedence over tailoring the course for professional practice doctoral students.

Adhering to the College of Education's research policy, Cohort 1 students took two quantitative research courses and a qualitative research course originally designed for Ph.D. students and taught by our research methods faculty, and one practitioner inquiry course designed for the Ed.D. program by our TSS program area faculty. This four-course sequence did not provide enough support for conducting research within our students' contexts, so we added a Foundations of Research course to the first semester of our program. Although institutional policy did not permit this course's consideration as research preparation, we developed it to orient our students to diverse ways of thinking about and conducting research, particularly as practitioner-scholars. Not surprisingly, the content, structure, and pedagogy across these five courses varied widely, as did the linkages instructors made to the rest of the program, to CPED principles and concepts, and to the students' professional lives.

We recognized that our task was to facilitate changes in the content and focus of the research courses carefully while maintaining collegial relationships with our colleagues from Research and Evaluation Methods. Over the course of 5 years, we met repeatedly with our research methodology colleagues with the goal of shaping the content of research courses so that all of them could be relevant and useful for our practitioner-scholars. While we respected our colleagues' knowledge of quantitative methodologies, we diverged on the notion that all practitioner-scholars needed to be able to design and conduct large quasi-experimental studies. We held firmly to the idea that practitioners could study their own contexts with rigor and generate local knowledge to affect immediate change. Furthermore, we were hoping (and unfortunately failing) to create coherence toward the values of equity and social justice, as well as the legitimacy of practitioner research. The disconnect was palpable.

We concluded that the only way to achieve flexibility in research preparation was to alter the College of Education's research policy, so we could gain control of research preparation within our own program area. Thus, we began our work with our college's Faculty Policy Council to revise its language. Within 5 months, we rallied enough support among the members of the Council to revise the research requirements for Ed.D. students. The new policy continued to require a 12-hour minimum of research preparation while permitting online Ed.D. programs to define a wider range of courses to satisfy those 12 hours. We celebrated this liberating policy shift while recovering from the occasionally contentious conversations with Ph.D.-habituated colleagues (Adams et al., 2014). This course of action moved us toward implementation by allowing us to redefine or restructure the innovation (Rogers, 2003) by removing institutional barriers.

This new freedom allowed us to (re)create research preparation to serve our students and their communities better, to represent our program values and goals, and to question and redefine what counts as research. We were able to move away from courses that privileged research conducted by university experts and move toward courses that challenged our students and provided them research skills and knowledge to address equity and justice in their contexts. Presently our TSS program has designed and taught five of our own specialized research courses and have a strong relationship with the instructor of the sixth course, a course still housed in the Research Methodology program area focused on reading and evaluating quantitative research, redesigned to meet the needs of practitioner scholars. The five TSS Ed.D. courses are interdependent and were built using core CPED principles and design concepts, including the framing of research around equity and social justice in order to systematically study problems of practice and enact change in local contexts. Importantly, we did not simply redesign research courses to study issues of equity through traditional research methods but instead with a focus on questioning and re-conceptualizing what counts as research and the types of research in which practitioner-scholars engage.

Programmatic Innovation

The six research preparation courses in the TSS Ed.D. program that we developed collectively and continue to refine through design-based research include Foundations of Research (Semester 1), Practitioner Inquiry 1 (Semester 2), Qualitative Research for Practitioner-Scholars (Semester 3), Quantitative Research for Practitioner-Scholars (Semester 4), Practitioner Inquiry 2 (Semester 5), and Designing Research (Semester 7). For each course, we describe its situation within the program along with objectives and specific innovations.

Foundations of Research in Curriculum and Instruction

The foundational course on research in curriculum and instruction is one of the first two courses students take in the program. This hybrid course occurs during the first summer of the program and meets online with one face-to-face session during the summer institute on campus. The course introduces students to educational scholarship through the lens of a professional practice doctoral degree. We find that our Ed.D. students enter our program with a very traditional, formulaic view of research: disconnected from teachers' realities, generated by experts, and utilized to evaluate K–12 students' abilities and teacher effectiveness using standardized measures. While our students can identify challenges in their contexts, they often imagine solutions as control-group studies to isolate variables and measure impact in terms of quantitative test results. Our goal in this course is to broaden mindsets by introducing them to humanizing research methods, building the foundation for their self-identification as practitioner-scholars. Students explore seminal and contemporary research in the field of curriculum and instruction; concepts and processes of educational research; practices of reading, analyzing, and critiquing scholarly literature; varieties of research methodologies and methods; and principles of academic writing. Humanizing research methods undergird these objectives via texts devoted to equity and justice-oriented research (e.g., Kuntz, 2016; Strunk & Locke, 2019). Students consider (mis)conceptions of what counts as research and the role of scholarly literature in addressing problems of practice in their contexts. Overall, we approach this course as a process-oriented exploration of practitioner scholarship and all it entails as we begin the work of preparing students to "construct and apply knowledge to make a positive difference in the lives of individuals, families, organizations, and communities" (CPED, n.d., Guiding Principle #2).

Practitioner Research: Theory and Practice (Practitioner Inquiry 1)

Following the broad overview of education research methods offered in the Foundations course, Practitioner Inquiry: Theory and Practice is strategically placed early in our doctoral students' program of studies (Semester 2). In this course, we develop students' basic knowledge of the practitioner inquiry movement, its history and theoretical underpinnings, as well as what it means to study one's own professional practice to enact change and contribute to the knowledge base about teaching and learning as a practitioner-scholar (Dana & Yendol-Hoppey, 2020). We frame equity as the ultimate "why" of engagement in practitioner inquiry as students gain practice in naming, framing, and studying a problem of practice as they complete a modest inquiry cycle to apply the knowledge and skills introduced in the course. In this course, students recognize themselves and fellow educators as potential producers of knowledge. They apply their learning by creating a presentation for their school or district to pitch the value of practitioner inquiry as a mechanism for teacher and administrator professional development, school improvement, and reform. Finally, they engage in a mini-cycle of inquiry in their contexts and share their learning in a course presentation.

This was the first research course developed specifically for the Ed.D. students when our program was launched in 2010. As such, it was an important innovation in and of itself. As it became clear through study of our program that our students needed data analysis experience prior to the DiP, we created a data analysis simulation, enabling students to practice analysis using another practitioner's data and compare their analysis with that of the actual practitioner researcher. In addition, we created a 10-minute video[2] and added it to the course in 2016 to exemplify the data analysis process for the practitioner researcher, featuring two of our program's graduates. Seeing and hearing other practitioner scholars engage in research helps our students build their confidence and identity as practitioner-scholars themselves.

Qualitative Research for Practitioner Scholars

This introductory qualitative research course, designed specifically for our Ed.D. students, is strategically situated after their Practitioner Inquiry 1 course and before the Quantitative Research course. We argue the types of questions generated by scholarly practitioners link inexorably to finding answers using qualitative research methods and methodology.

Prior courses taught by our qualitative methodology colleagues explained the foundations of qualitative methods, focusing on some of the more complex and intensive methods such as grounded theory and phenomenology. Since we prepare our students to conduct research in rapidly changing educational environments, those methods were not helpful, so we designed a qualitative research course focused on methods more likely to find use in shorter cycles of inquiry. We knew we had to first shift mindsets that privileged objective quantitative methods, and then we needed to teach and practice the skills of qualitative inquiry. In this course, we ask students to consider their own subjectivities as people and professionals. Asking students to state their positionality scaffolds them through processes in recognizing the ways in which their social positions inform their reactions to who, what, how, and why they teach—and even what they choose to inquire about as practitioner researchers. This inward reflection at the individual and collective level "provides opportunities for candidates to develop and demonstrate collaboration and communication skills to work with diverse communities and to build partnerships" (CPED n.d., Guiding Principle #3).

Quantitative Methods for Evaluation in Educational Environments

This course follows the Qualitative Research course and is similarly designed to be responsive to the needs of practitioner-scholars. The purpose of the course is to build an understanding of the common descriptive and inferential statistics used to inform educational policy and funding decisions that influence educational efforts in schools and other learning environments. As practitioner-scholars, our graduates would lead change informed by research and therefore need to be able to assess the quality of the studies and implications of their findings. Required readings included practitioner-oriented texts (e.g., Frey, 2016), as well as exemplars of educational research that included topics such as retention of STEM teachers (Horvath et al., 2018) and college success of students from low-income backgrounds (Castleman et al., 2014).

Practitioner Research: Data Collection and Analysis (Practitioner Inquiry II)

After having qualitative and quantitative research methodologies during semesters 3 and 4, students return to practitioner inquiry in semester 5. This course revisits many concepts introduced in the first practitioner inquiry class, deepening initial understandings related to studying one's own professional practice by synthesizing the content of the qualitative and quantitative research classes and applying the research skills learned in these classes to the work of a practitioner-researcher. This course focuses on helping students to solidify the relationship between studying their own professional practice and creating more just and equitable schooling experiences for adults and students in their local contexts. As part of this critical work, we frame this course around "questions of equity, ethics, and social justice to bring about solutions to complex problems of practice" (CPED, n.d., Guiding Principle #1). Through inquiry-based recursive learning experiences (CPED, n.d., Guiding Principle #5), a primary course outcome is to cultivate the skills of a practitioner-scholar through advanced study of practitioner inquiry and its utility within their daily work as educators and in preparation for the DiP.

During the second half of the course, students complete a modest practitioner research study where, working in small groups, they practice data analysis skills by exploring whom they are becoming as practitioner-scholars committed to more just and equitable schooling experiences for the children and adults they serve. This cycle of inquiry is innovative as it connects the content of two courses—this and a course titled Critical Pedagogy from earlier in the program of study—to provide a common set of data for students to analyze as they continue to practice data analysis skills. In contrast to the inquiry cycle students completed in the first Practitioner Research course, which focused on an individual problem of practice, this cycle focuses all of our students on the most pervasive problem of practice all practitioner-scholars face in schools today: the creation of more just and equitable schooling experiences. Finally, this inquiry cycle purposefully engages our students in self-study of their own emerging practitioner-scholar identities, preparing them well for the DiP experience (Dana et al., 2021).

Conceptualizing Research in Curriculum and Instruction

We developed this course after realizing that each of us was still doing an incredible amount of scaffolding for our advisees when they planned their dissertations. We needed a course that provided structures and supports to conceptualize research around their individual problems of practice to prepare for the DiP. In this course, students begin by examining dissertation proposals from our Ed.D. graduates, discussing what they noticed and raising questions about the process. Then, students move through each major element of the DiP proposal, including articulating a problem of practice, drafting research question(s), learning from relevant literature, determining preliminary research methods, developing trustworthiness, and stating their positionality. Each of these processes explicitly connects to students' unique contexts. As such, this course relies on "field-based opportunities to analyze problems of practice and use[s] multiple frames to develop meaningful solutions" (CPED, n.d., Guiding Principle #4). Students finish the course with a dissertation proposal brief as they move into their qualifying examination preparation.

Impact on Practitioner Scholars and their Communities

Current students and graduates alike report that experiencing innovative research processes throughout the program enabled them to enact change in their local contexts. Many of our students' DiPs center on "real-world dilemmas" involving marginalized students or groups (Ma et al., 2018). In the final chapter of the DiP, our students describe an action plan for using findings to make change in their local contexts. Typically, this plan includes steps for the researcher and others, including school-based colleagues, district-level administrators, professional development departments, community organizations, families, and teacher preparation programs. Evidence from DiPs shows that our programmatic innovation has implications for classroom practice, school-wide initiatives, and local and state professional organizations (Dana et al., 2016). Our graduates describe being proactive in identifying and addressing local dilemmas, including the improvement of teaching and learning (Kennedy et al., 2019). This evidence demonstrates how work in our program extends beyond online coursework, summer institutes, qualifying exams, and DiPs. Indeed, the multi-faceted and equity-focused work of our students often has immediate and lasting effects on their classrooms, schools, communities, and beyond.

Coda: Reflections and New Challenges

Reflecting on our program helps us continue *clarifying* and then *routinizing* our innovation (Rogers, 2003). By studying the experiences and impacts of our graduates, we learn more about how the elements of our program and our research preparation have supported their work, and we adjust accordingly. We continue to engage in CPED, sharing our work, pushing our own thinking, and adapting to the ever-changing educational landscape.

As we reflected on our innovation at the time we crafted our CPED Program of the Year Award application as well as wrote this chapter, we identified more challenges at our research-intensive university context. The rules of the Graduate School govern our program, putting parameters on the dissertation structure and elements, and more importantly, on who can serve as dissertation chairs and committee members for our students. Currently, we must have four committee members (including the chair), each having earned Graduate Faculty Status (GFS) at our institution. To earn GFS at the University of Florida, faculty must have a strong record of publication and a history of mentoring students in research. We cannot include respected practitioner-scholars in the community on committees, and even brand-new faculty can face years of waiting to get the experience and publications they need to earn GFS. While we continue to be proud of our restructured three-chapter dissertation and our reclaiming of what counts as research courses, advisor and committee membership being restricted to only faculty who have GFS limits our ability to grow our program, as there are only so many faculty with GFS who understand practitioner scholarship and are committed to advising Ed.D. students. Further, these restrictions rob our university faculty and students of the opportunity for respected and knowledgeable practicing professionals to offer their unique perspectives and expertise to the DiP experience. Finally, our Graduate School's parameters on the dissertation structure and elements affect our ability to innovate dissertation format outside the Graduate School norm (i.e., collaborative group-written dissertations). These are the next innovations we must address.

In addition to this new innovation journey, we are faced with a new problem of practice that has emerged recently as legislation in our own state (and beyond) forbids the use of state funds to support diversity and equity initiatives and programs. Our program's problem of practice has become navigating the tensions developing between expectations for an equity-focused dissertation-in-practice and the immense pressure our students are experiencing in their school and classroom contexts to avoid equity work. We wonder:

- Will we face external pressures to change the social justice focus of our award-winning program?
- Will our students be able to research the topics for which they are so passionate?
- How might our research courses, our students' research board approvals, and dissertation committee composition need to be adapted to address these tensions?

So far, we remain relatively free of excessive pressure to change our program courses and content. The political lens focuses mostly on K–12 schooling experiences and developmental appropriateness. With our program situated at the doctoral level, with students who seek the social justice focus we espouse, we have had no complaints by students that often trigger media attention. However, we are working to understand the impact of current legislation on the students we serve and are uncertain of what the future holds.

Yet, we remain optimistic and continue to keep our mission and values clearly outlined on our program website. Affiliation with CPED and the values they espouse lends support to our steadfast commitment to equity and social justice in our Ed.D. program. As we explore these new challenges, our Ed.D. program, and the research courses within it, will continue to evolve. We look forward to the next iteration of innovation, as we embrace innovation as our perpetual state of being, rather than a one-time award and achievement.

Endnotes

1. It was the recipient of the 2011 Program of the Year Award from the Association of Teacher Educators.
2. This video can be viewed at https://www.youtube.com/watch?v=yzo92E_Ew_8

References

Adams, A., Bondy, E., Ross, D., Dana, N. F., & Kennedy-Lewis, B. (2014). Implementing an online professional practice doctoral program in a Ph.D. environment: Managing the dilemmas. *Journal of School Public Relations, 35*(3), 363–382.

Andrews, R., & Grogan, M. (2005). Form should follow function: Removing the Ed.D. dissertation from the Ph.D. straight jacket. *UCEA Review, 46*(2), 10–12.

Auerbach, S. (2011). "It's not just going to collect dust on a shelf:" Faculty Perceptions of the Applied Dissertation in the New California State University (CSU) Ed. D. Programs Leadership Education from within a Feminist Ethos. *Journal of Research on Leadership Education, 6*(3), 59–82.

Castleman, B. L., Page, L. C., & Schooley, K. (2014). The forgotten summer: Does the offer of college school graduates? *Journal of Policy Analysis and Management, 33*(2), 320–344. doi.org/10.1002/pam.21743

Cochran-Smith, M., & Lytle, S. (1993) *Inside/Outside: Teacher Research and Knowledge.* Teachers College Press.

CPED. (n.d.). *The CPED framework.* https://www.cpedinitiative.org/the-framework

Dana, N. F., Bondy, E., Kennedy-Lewis, B., Adams, A., & Ma, V. W. (2016). Exemplifying the dissertation in practice. Carnegie Project on the Education Doctorate (CPED) White Paper Project. http://www.cpedinitiative.org/research-resources

Dana, N. F., & Yendol-Hoppey, D. (2020). *The reflective educator's guide to classroom research: Learning to teach and teaching to learn through practitioner inquiry.* Corwin Press.

Dana, N. F., Rigney, J., Ma, V. W., & Vescio, V. (2021). Project-based learning and doctoral student research skill development: A case study. *Impacting Education: Journal on Transforming Professional Practice, 6*(4), 27–35. https://doi.org/10.5195/ie.2021.148

Frey, B. B. (2016). *There's a stat for THAT!* Sage Publications.

Horvath, M., Goodell, J. E., & Kosteas, V. D. (2018). Decisions to enter and continue in the teaching profession: Evidence from a sample of U.S. secondary STEM teacher candidates. *Teaching and Teacher Education, 71*, 57–65. https://psycnet.apa.org/doi/10.1016/j.tate.2017.12.007

Kennedy, B. L., Bondy, E., Dana, N. F., Vescio, V., & Ma, V. (2019). The development and enactment of practitioner scholarship among graduates from one online Ed.D. programme. *Journal of Further and Higher Education, 44*(5), 653–669. https://doi.org/10.1080/0309877X.2019.1576858

Kuntz, A. M. (2016). *The responsible methodologist: Inquiry, truth-telling, and social justice.* Routledge.

Lave, J. & Wenger, E. (1991). *Situated learning: Legitimate peripheral participation.* Cambridge University Press.

Ma, V. W., Dana, N. F., Adams, A., & Kennedy, B. L. (2018). Understanding the problem of practice: An analysis of professional practice Ed.D. dissertations. *Impacting Education: Journal on Transforming Professional Practice, 3*(1), 13–22.

McDonald, J. P., Mohr, N., Dichter, A., & McDonald, E. C. (2013). *The power of protocols: An educator's guide to better practice, 3rd edition.* Teachers College Press.

Rogers, E. M. (2003). *Diffusion of innovations* (5th ed.). Free Press.

Strunk, K. K., & Locke, L. A. (Eds.). (2019). *Research methods for social justice and equity in education.* Palgrave Macmillan.

Wang, F., & Hannafin, M. J. (2005). Design-based research and technology-enhanced learning environments. *Educational Technology Research and Development, 53*(4), 5–23.

CHAPTER SEVEN

Innovation and Excellence in Baylor University's Ed.D. in Learning and Organizational Change

NICHOLAS R. WERSE, ELIZABETH ANNE MURRAY, SANDI COOPER, LAILA SANGURAS, AND LACY CROCKER PAPADAKIS

In 2018, a team of educators in Baylor University's Department of Curriculum and Education came together to redefine its educational doctorate in a way that expanded the concept of an "educator" to fields beyond early childhood, K–12, and higher education. Recognizing the importance of education in every profession, the program's leadership designed the Ed.D. in Learning and Organizational Change (Ed.D.-LOC), an educational doctorate seeking to "champion systemic change across schools, government agencies, businesses, and private organizations" (Baylor University, para. 1). Within 4 years of its inception, the Ed.D.-LOC program has become Baylor University's largest and most diverse online doctoral program, with over 500 total students, 59% of whom are students of color and 30% of whom come from industries outside traditional education fields. To support students with this diverse array of backgrounds and professional experiences, we built a highly innovative student support system (Blevins et al., 2021; Shelton et al., 2023; Werse, 2021; Werse et al., 2022). Throughout this process, we employed a robust assortment of program evaluation strategies that allowed us to collect real-time data and make strategic and targeted programmatic changes to improve student outcomes continually.

This combination of innovation, program evaluation, and adaptability eventually led to our receipt of CPED's Program of the Year Award for 2022. While this award brought national recognition to our program, it also prompted reflection about how best to sustain programmatic strengths that the award recognized. Using the language of Rogers' (2003) diffusion of innovation theory, the award corresponded with a moment in our program's development in which we shifted our attention more intentionally toward the final element needed to sustain our program's operations: routinizing.

In this chapter, we describe the development of Baylor's Ed.D.-LOC program, focusing on two innovative design features: the expanded concept of education across professions and a multi-layered system of student supports for online scholar-practitioners. In keeping with this volume's theoretical framework, we use Rogers' (2003) diffusion of innovation theory to frame the stages in our program's development. We present this reflection in three parts. First, using Rogers' agenda-setting, matching, and redefining/restructuring stages, we look at innovations that occurred during the program's early development and design as well as their compatibility and relative advantages. During this time, we utilized internal data to consider how our program equitably responded to the diverse backgrounds, goals, and needs of our students. In the second section, we utilize Rogers' clarifying stage as a frame to discuss the reflective process that occurred as we applied for the CPED Program of the Year Award. The process of applying for the award pushed program leaders to consider how we observed, captured, and measured program impact in communities beyond the traditional graduate school metrics. In the third section, we reflect upon how winning the CPED Program of the Year Award has influenced our program's self-perception and operations. Although receiving the award is a recent development for our program, we have already seen changes in our alumni engagement, student recruitment, and faculty searches. Programmatically, winning the award pushed us to devote more attention to considering how to sustain the high quality of our innovations—a development best characterized by Rogers' fifth stage, routinizing.

Agenda-setting, Matching, & Restructuring: The Early Development of the Baylor Ed.D.-LOC

Our story began with a small Ed.D. program that resembled a slightly lighter manifestation of the corresponding Ph.D. program in Baylor's Department of Curriculum and Instruction. The Ed.D. and Ph.D. students often enrolled in the same classes and completed similarly structured dissertations. With low enrollments, we discussed the possibility of moving the Ed.D. online with an Online Program Manager to reach a broader range of students. This process best reflects our program's operations in the agenda-setting stage of Rogers' (2003) diffusion of innovation theory. From these conversations, we realized the potential of relaunching our Ed.D. as a completely re-envisioned terminal degree program for scholar-practitioners.

We formed a strategic planning committee—called the "Think Tank"—to guide the restructuring process and identified the Carnegie Project on the Education Doctorate (2019; see also Buss & Zambo, 2014; Perry, 2013; Schuster, 2017) framework as the ideal articulation of foundational principles upon which to structure the program. The CPED framework provided helpful language to design a practitioner-focused program that blurred the lines between traditionally bifurcated "scholarly" and "practitioner" degree programs (see also the discussion in Piantanida et al., 2018). We wanted to avoid the stigma of the Ed.D. as a "Ph.D. lite" (Allen et al., 2016, p. 105). In this process, we found the many CPED-inspired publications reflecting on how other institutions developed their programs to be very helpful (e.g., George, 2017; Peterson, 2017).

In addition to the CPED framework, we sought insight into the nuances of moving a program online. As none of our faculty had taught in an online program, we realized that we needed guidance from those who had. To this end, we found Kumar and Dawson's (2018) reflections on their experiences launching an Ed.D. in educational technology at the University of Florida particularly helpful (see also Chapman & Jackson, 2021). We also benefited from the emerging scholarly discussions about mentoring doctoral students in online programs (e.g., Banks, 2018; Hyder & Gilliam, 2015).

From its earliest conception, three goals laid the foundation for our program's innovation. Each of these goals matched the needs we identified in the original Ed.D. program and addressed the challenges of going online. First, we aimed to maximize the program's accessibility to a diverse student body of working professionals across industry sectors, geographical regions, and ethnic backgrounds. The commitment to program accessibility aligned with both the CPED framework (Principle 1) and Baylor University's strategic plan, titled *Illuminate* (Baylor University, 2018, Pillar 1). Our reasons for pursuing a more inclusive program were twofold. First, the Ed.D. aims to empower change in education communities, and we saw the value of broadening the idea of "education" as a vehicle for change management to include other industry leaders seeking an advanced degree to support intra-industry leadership and organizational change efforts.[1] Second, building on our core conviction that diversity adds richness to educational spaces, we worked to create student cohorts that embodied different voices, beliefs, and opinions. In learning from one another throughout the program, we built bridges for our graduates to establish ongoing community and industry partnerships, joining together in the ever-present mission of making our living and working communities safer, more equitable places (CPED Principle 2, 4, 5, & 6 and Baylor University, 2018, Pillar 2).

This commitment informed the decision to offer the program online, the structuring of the admissions process to remove inequitable barriers (such as the GRE), as well as the design of the student support systems to be customizable based on the unique needs of each student. To encourage institutional and organizational diversity within the program, we designed the admissions process to prioritize practice-based leadership experience. We require a minimum of 3 years in industry leadership to ensure that scholarly practitioners enter the program as seasoned leaders in their fields who seek to engage with colleagues as a community of practice and grow in their respective industries.

This commitment to structuring a program to maximize accessibility across industry sectors proved immediately successful. From the program's launch in 2018 to the writing of this chapter, the student body reflected diverse industries (See Figure 7.1). Half of students serve in K–12 education, 19% in higher education, 7% in corporate and business sectors, 7% in mental healthcare, 5% in the military, 4% in health care, 4% in nonprofits, 3% in government service, and 1% in educational administration. Thus, 31% of current scholarly practitioners in the program come from outside the traditional field of "education" to obtain training in education and leadership principles to empower their organizational change efforts within their respective industries (CPED Principles 2 & 6, Baylor University, 2018, Pillar 2). The breadth of industry experience results in considerable diversity in student research foci across cohorts and enriches the student experience, as they learn to examine problems across disciplines and sectors. In addition to industry diversity, the program consists of 59% students of color and 41% instructors of color, making it one of the most diverse at Baylor. Students and faculty repeatedly note that this industry and racial diversity contribute to the unique and rich learning community in the program (Lively et al., 2021)

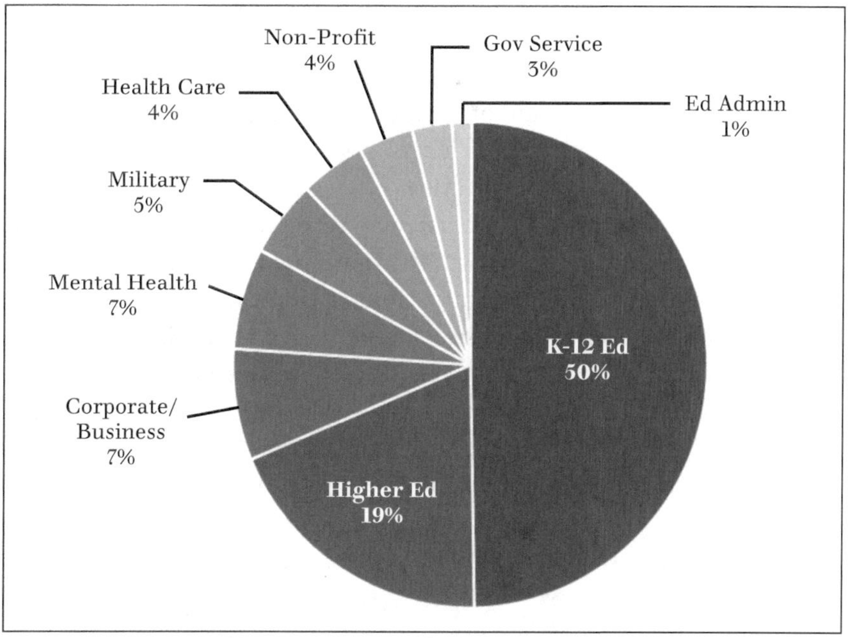

Figure 7.1. Baylor Ed.D.-LOC Scholarly Practitioner Industry Sector Research Foci

The second goal was our desire to equip diverse scholarly practitioners to lead social justice and equity-oriented change initiatives in their industries outside of academia while speaking to the traditional graduate-level academic metrics set by our aspiring R1 university.[2] We designed this program in the space between two sets of institutional values that influenced the development of the Ed.D.-LOC's curriculum, assessments, and student support systems. First, we identified the CPED framework as the ideal model from which to construct a practitioner-oriented, terminal degree program that focused on equipping industry leaders to address problems of professional practice (CPED Principles 3–5). We structured the course sequence to frame questions of professional practice around issues of equity, ethics, and social justice (CPED Principle 1) and to emphasize collaborative leadership in industry practice (CPED Principles 2 & 3). We aimed to equip scholarly practitioners for leading strategic change initiatives in their industries, organizations, and communities that improve equitable access to services and address social justice concerns within the industry (CPED Principle 2). The CPED framework provided the foundational principles upon which we designed the vertical and horizontal alignment of the course sequence, assessments, and outcomes, ensuring each piece contributed to the achievement of the larger goal.

In addition to the CPED Framework, we operated within the context of, what was at the time, an aspiring R1 university that measured terminal degree outcomes through traditional academic metrics for research production (e.g., publications, research funding, and dissertation production). Baylor's *Illuminate Academic Strategic Plan* defined four Pillars foundational for Baylor's attainment of R-1 status within 5 years: Baylor's "Christian Environment," "Transformational Education," "Research and Scholarship," and "Arts and Athletics." Baylor's Christian commitment to a caring community undergirds the university's efforts toward improving equitable access to education, increasing institutional diversity, and pioneering inclusive educational spaces.

Designing a practitioner-focused program within this context provided an ideal environment for us to present scholarly-practitioner leadership and change initiatives outside of the academy as a recognizable part of the academy's graduate-level knowledge production process to university stakeholders. By combining the focus of CPED Principle 1 and Baylor University's (2018) *Illuminate* Pillar 1, we oriented many of these outcomes around questions of equity, ethics, and social justice in professional practice. We recognized that while traditional metrics of academic writing outcomes are valuable, we wanted to acknowledge scholarly practitioner contributions to the knowledge by way of leading contextualized changes in their industries, organizations, and professional practice (CPED Principles 5 & 6).

The third goal for our program was the commitment to a highly adaptive and customizable student support system to meet the unique needs of adult learners. When we designed the Ed.D.-LOC program, Baylor had few online programs and little institutional infrastructure to support such programs. As such, departments launching online programs often contracted outside support or built an internal administrative infrastructure. We saw this unprecedented task as what Rogers (2003) termed a "relative advantage" (p. 15), which prompted us to create a highly responsive leadership system that adapted to student needs. We created a series of data collection systems that allowed us to measure student outcomes and respond to student feedback as we improved the program. In addition to course evaluations and periodic student experience surveys, we designed a database in which the Research and Writing Development Center (RWDC) tracks student dissertation progress. With these data, the Think Tank made iterative program adjustments to improve the student experience and educational outcomes.

The resulting program proved remarkably successful, as one of the first challenges we faced was how to scale the program far beyond initial enrollment projections. Although we planned for 15–30 students per cohort, the first cohort consisted of 58 students with subsequent cohorts enrolling between 50 and 90 students. To support students coming from a range of professional, academic, racial, ethnic, and geographical backgrounds, we developed our innovative student support system consisting of an advising team to guide students as they progressed in the course sequence and navigate the myriad of university resources. These resources included the RWDC, designed specifically to work with online doctoral students as they wrote their dissertations-in-practice (Werse, 2021; Werse et al., 2022). Having successfully moved through agenda setting to matching, our program completed the initiation stage of the broader innovation process (Rogers, 2003) and, with the collection of early data, we entered the implementation stage where we could pause to reflect on the original goals and the systems and solutions we implemented to address them.

Clarifying: Measuring Outcomes and Telling Our Story through the CPED Program of the Year Application

While a fair amount of redefining and restructuring took place in the shift from an on-the-ground program to an online platform, a new phase of redefining and restructuring began to occur as the program produced its first graduates. Because the program was growing, we wanted to ensure that the systems we put into place not only adapted vertically to students as they progressed through the program but also horizontally as the number of cohorts expanded each trimester. We recognized the program's successes and considered applying for the CPED Program of the Year Award, but also recognized the need to ensure that our data collection systems captured data that spoke to the CPED framework and the Program of the Year Award goals. Thus began the clarifying stage as we continued in the broader activity of implementation (Rogers, 2003).

Because we wanted a highly responsive program, we designed several instruments to track student experiences throughout the process. These instruments served as channels of communication through which we could measure the success of our students and program at multiple points and from varying perspectives. We already had student course evaluations, student experience surveys, and an exit survey. Additionally, because the student success team and the RWDC had frequent engagement with students throughout the program, we designed a system for them to report their engagement with students as well as the facilitators of and obstacles to student success that they encountered.

Having a program based on the CPED framework, much of the data we collected already aligned well with the CPED Program of the Year Award criteria. For example, we tracked the impact of the program's emphasis on preparing scholarly practitioners to lead social justice and equity-oriented change efforts (CPED Principle 1, Baylor University, 2018, Pillar 4). Indeed, two-thirds of all Problem of Practice dissertations explicitly engaged questions related to diversity, inclusion, equity, and social justice. Furthermore, exit survey data (n = 133) revealed that on a scale from 1–3 (with 3 being "very supportive"), graduates ranked faculty and staff exceptionally high at 2.79 and their classmates at 2.85. These data reveal the depth of community experienced by students during their time in the program.

The process of assessing these data for the CPED Program of the Year Award application, however, provided an exceptional opportunity to reflect upon the types of data collected and the intended purposes of those data. All data collection systems need a purpose and a plan to answer a specific set of questions. Thus, when we approached the data through the lens of the CPED Program of the Year Award application. We identified ways that we could adjust the data collection systems to improve their precision and accuracy while expanding the versatility of the data.

While we had substantive data on student experiences within the program, we realized that we had fewer systems capturing student impact outside of the program, such as when they assumed new leadership roles, launched organizational change initiatives, published, presented at conferences, or received awards. This matter becomes further complicated when tracking alumni's impact on their communities. Because our program's innovation centers on expanding the breadth of the Ed.D. into diverse industries, what accounts for success for one student may look different for another. In the Problem of Practice Dissertation topics alone, our students' work range greatly. Topics included the application of andragogy principles to increase employee engagement and retention in IT (Walker-Schmidt et al., 2022), age-related discrimination in the workplace (Franz et al., 2022), playground accessibility for differently-abled children (Bunn et al., 2022), disciplinary disparities in primary education (Yeung, 2022), and the formation of professional learning communities to support district improvement (Bowman, 2021). The industry diversity of our students helps to make our program successful, but it also requires innovative metrics for assessment. To meet this need early in the program's development, we designed the *Luminaries Report*, providing a central venue for students, faculty, and alumni to report their leadership initiatives, promotions, awards, grants, honors, publications, and presentations that occur outside of the program. The *Luminaries Report* proved immensely helpful when applying for the CPED Program of the Year Award, allowing us to speak to the program's impact beyond the student experience.

The process of adjusting the scope of our data collection capabilities expanded our ability to tell our program's story both on the CPED Program of the Year Award as well as to stakeholders within our university. Most of our students (66%) report career developments in the form of a new position, promotion, or leadership opportunity during their time in the program. In the last year, Ed.D.-LOC students and alumni wrote 32 publications, gave 67 conference presentations, and received 29 awards or grants for their leadership and research. Of these, 24 publications and 41 presentations explicitly engaged questions of equity, ethics, and social justice (CPED Principle 1; Baylor University, 2018, Pillar 1). The program's greatest impact came through the leadership initiatives of its students and alumni. Student leadership metrics reveal that 76% of the first two graduating cohorts ($n = 84$) held mid-level, senior-level, or community leadership positions at the time of graduation. The industry diversity of our students means that our scholarly practitioners advance to a wide range of sectors and positions.

Routinizing: Looking Forward After Receiving the Award

Winning the Program of the Year award highlighted the success of our efforts to build a program aligned with the CPED principles. On the one hand, winning the award has led to increased visibility both within the CPED community and across our university networks. The leaders of several institutions approached us after our CPED Program of the Year Award reception presentation to discuss various aspects of our program and ways in which we navigated the aforementioned challenges. Since winning the award, program leaders received multiple invitations to publish on various aspects of our innovations (e.g., Kaul & Sanguras, 2023; Shelton et al., 2023; Werse et al., 2023) and *Fortune Magazine* featured our program. Furthermore, because writing development is such a core part of our program, we additionally presented at the 2022 CPED convening on the facilitators and obstacles to students achieving doctoral candidacy (Kaul et al., 2022). After this presentation, we had leaders from several programs reach out to learn more about our RWDC. We additionally presented on our unique approach to writing development support at the International Writing Centers Association, which generated interest from other writing center professionals (Crocker Papadakis, Kaul, Davis, et al., 2022; Crocker Papadakis, Kaul, Werse, et al., 2022).

On the other hand, this increased recognition has led to reflections on how best to routinize (Rogers, 2003) the strengths of our program and stabilize program operations to ensure the sustainability of our team. The faculty and staff in the Ed.D.-LOC program are leaders with expertise that ranges across industries. Knowing this, we wanted to create a structure to allow for engagement in their areas of interest, while also providing opportunities for input and buy-in. To accomplish this goal, we created a system of faculty governance that allows all members of faculty *and* staff to contribute to the decision-making processes of the department. Faculty and staff each serve on one of five committees: Alumni and Development, Course Development and Curriculum, Research and Publications, Strategic Planning and Future Directions, and Student Experience. This structure has created a routinized and equitable process for faculty and staff to be involved actively in programmatic decision-making.

We have also created a replicable structure for how faculty teach the Problem of Practice (PoP) dissertation courses. Throughout the program, students take four PoP courses (see description in Blevins et al., 2021); these courses are taught by a team of faculty advisors that rotates every term. Each term, the materials evolved as we recognized the different needs of our students. While we always focus on continuous improvement, we have reached a point where our materials only need refreshing rather than a complete redesign. This creates space for faculty to focus on meeting regularly and providing feedback to students on their writing rather than recreating course materials.

Our dissertation committee structure has also evolved to include regular reviews and input from the entire committee, which consists of two faculty members and a member of the RWDC. Before this evolution, the faculty advisor and a member of the RWDC read the document to determine whether a student met the expectations of the program; the additional faculty member read the document just before the defense in term nine. In a fast-paced program of our size, we realized that students would be more successful if they received feedback from their entire committee as early as possible. We have now moved the entire committee review to terms five and eight, with a final review before the defense in term nine. Changing this structure also created an opportunity for us to consider the role of each member of the committee. While the Faculty Advisor directs the content, coherence, method, and outcomes of the study, the second reader checks each section of the document to ensure that all needed content is present to meet program requirements. The third reader then provides feedback on the overall writing flow, coherence, and alignment, in addition to providing feedback on the document's APA and formatting.

Similarly, faculty have worked together to clarify "what counts" for a Baylor Ed.D. Problem of Practice dissertation (on this topic more broadly, see Lovitts, 2007). For example, we have determined the type and quantity of data that students must collect and analyze for qualitative, quantitative, and mixed methods designs. By establishing these distinctions, faculty advisors can confidently and consistently advise their students. We curated a bank of outlines for students to use when writing up the results chapters of their dissertations to standardize the expectations. This standardization also ensures that every member of a student's committee provides feedback aligned with program expectations (Gillham et al., 2019).

Coda

The affirmation of a prestigious award from a national organization solidified our standing as a leading Ed.D. program. This recognition not only highlighted our program on campus, but it also demonstrated that while an Ed.D. program has more of a practitioner focus, the research and dissertation outcomes are just as rigorous as a Ph.D. program. In many respects, winning this award has served to make the relative advantages of our programmatic innovations more visible to stakeholders beyond our program. It has shone a light on the inherent systems we designed to ensure we tried, tested, assessed, and modified innovations to ensure optimal outcomes for students. This process, while not perfectly aligning with Rogers' (2003) diffusion of innovation theory at all stages in our program's history, maps well onto many of the broad categories that Rogers developed for understanding the diffusion of innovations throughout an organization or industry.

Although prospective students seek the Ed.D.-LOC program because of the reputation of the university, this national recognition has heightened the distinctive qualities of the program that promotes recruitment of high-quality students. The award has played a pivotal role in prospective student interest, making the program more competitive and a desired top choice for an online Ed.D. program.

As the program continues to grow, there has been an increased need for hiring faculty who embody the scholar-practitioner, leadership experience, and commitment we seek to cultivate among our students. Receiving this national recognition has transformed the motivation prospective faculty have for joining the program. Whereas at the beginning of this program, prospective faculty were drawn to the convenience of teaching remotely at a reputable university, after receiving this national recognition, prospective faculty are now more interested in being a part of an innovative program.

After receiving this national recognition, alumni can now share they graduated from an awarding-winning graduate program, and they are more inclined to stay connected to maintain the association with a nationally recognized group of faculty and staff. The Ed.D.-LOC leadership team has organized special events to support this connection. Some of these events include an affinity group, which provides an organized mechanism for communication, participation in the homecoming parade and tailgate, and an active scholarship fund to encourage alumni to make small gifts back to the program to help current students with books, fees, and tuition. In addition to these events, program leaders stayed engaged with alumni by sending a customized mug and sticker soon after they graduate, a notecard in the mail with a bulleted list of ways to stay connected, and periodically, an alumni survey to gather feedback. At this time, program leaders are in the process of inviting alumni to be regional ambassadors, who will help connect current students and alumni through events in their cities or regions. In all these events, printed materials, and engagement, the message is clear that these alumni are from a nationally recognized Ed.D. program.

Programmatically, winning the CPED Program of the Year award pushed us to devote more attention to considering how to sustain the high quality of our innovations and continue to develop new ideas to support meaningful experiences for students and faculty. The process of applying for and receiving this award enhanced our programmatic ability for self-examination, making iterative improvements, increasing student recruitment, expanding faculty searches, and increasing alumni engagement.

Endnotes

1. See also the discussion on broadening the CPED framework in Arrows (2017).
2. On December 16, 2021, Baylor earned the designation of an R1 doctoral institution with "very high research activity" by the Carnegie Classification of Institutions of Higher Education. We conducted the program's planning and initial launch before Baylor achieved this designation. However, the university was committing considerable resource to attaining this designation.

References

Allen, J., Chirchello, M., & Wasicko, M. (2016). The practitioner-scholar doctorate: Not a PhD lite. In J. A. Perry (Ed.), *The EdD and the scholarly practitioner: The CPED path* (pp. 105–130). Information Age.

Arrows, F. (2017). Four ways to expand the foundation for CPED's social justice framework. *Impacting Education: Journal on Transforming Professional Practice, 2*(1), 28–32. https://doi.org/10.5195/ie.2017.28

Banks, K. L. (2018). Identifying online graduate learner's perceived barriers to their academic success. In A. G. Scheg & M. Shaw (Eds.), *Fostering effective communication in online graduate courses* (pp. 193–223). IGI Global.

Baylor University. (2018). *Illuminate* [Academic Strategic Plan]. https://illuminate.web.baylor.edu/

Blevins, B., Cooper, S., Crocker Papadakis, L., Earl, J., Howell, L., Lively, C., Meehan, J., Murray, E. A., Pratt, S., Sanguras, L., Talbert, S., Talbert, T. L., & Werse, N. R. (2021). Reframing the problem of practice: Transitions in Baylor University's Ed.D. in Learning and Organizational Change program. *Impacting Education: Journal on Transforming Professional Practice, 7*(1), 32–41. https://doi.org/10.5195/ie.2022.230

Bowman, M. (2021). Professional learning for a virtual world: Network helps districts navigate challenging times. *The Learning Professional, 42*(5), 42–46.

Bunn, T. D., Howell, L., & Crocker Papadakis, L. K. (2022). Fair play: A qualitative exploration of visitor behavior at Playgrand adventures all-abilities playground. *Impacting Education: Journal on Transforming Professional Practice, 7*(2), 39–50. https://doi.org/10.5195/ie.2022.206

Buss, R. R., & Zambo, D. (2014). *A practical guide for students and faculty in CPED-influenced programs working on an action research dissertation in practice.* Carnegie Project on the Education Doctorate.

Carnegie Project on the Education Doctorate. (2019). *Our vision and mission.* CPEDinitiative.Org. https://www.cpedinitiative.org/vision-mission

Chapman, L. A., & Jackson, A. M. (2021). Accessibility matters: Universal design and the online professional practice doctorate. *Impacting Education: Journal on Transforming Professional Practice, 6*(3), 1–6. https://doi.org/10.5195/ie.2021.184

Crocker Papadakis, L., Kaul, C., Davis, B. K., Werse, N. R., Smith, J., & Howell, L. (2022, October 26). *Strong connections: Relationship building between faculty and writing center professionals* [Conference Presentation].

Crocker Papadakis, L., Kaul, C., Werse, N. R., Smith, J., Davis, B. K., & Howell, L. (2022, October 26). *Graduate students' engagement with the writing center in an online doctoral program* [Conference Presentation]. International Writing Centers Association, Vancouver, BC, Canada.

Franz, N. E., Werse, N. R., & Talbert, T. L. (2022). Ageism-induced anxiety of job seekers aged 50–83: Preliminary findings from a phenomenological case study problem of practice dissertation. *Impacting Education: Journal on Transforming Professional Practice, 7*(2), 11–18. https://doi.org/10.5195/ie.2022.199

George, P. (2017). Toward a social justice model for an EdD program in higher education. *Impacting Education: Journal on Transforming Professional Practice, 2*(1). https://doi.org/10.5195/ie.2017.29

Gillham, J. C., Williams, N. V., Rife, G., & Parker, K. K. (2019). Problems of practice: A document analysis of education doctorate dissertations. *Impacting Education: Journal on Transforming Professional Practice, 4*(1), Article 1. https://doi.org/10.5195/ie.2019.85

Hyder, N., & Gilliam, J. (2015). How mentors can improve online graduate student attrition rates. *ELearn, 2015*(1). https://doi.org/10.1145/2721891.2724693

Kaul, C., & Sanguras, L. (2023). Intentionality and application of andragogy in EdD applied research courses to prepare students for a problem of practice dissertation. In C. Benedetti & A. Covarrubias (Eds.), *Teaching critical inquiry and applied research in Ed.D. programs moving beyond traditional methods*. Meyers Press.

Kaul, C., Werse, N. R., & Sanguras, L. Y. (2022, October 12). *Achieving doctoral candidacy: A study of scholar-practitioner perceptions of facilitators and obstacles when writing their problem of practice dissertation literature review and methodology* [Conference Presentation]. Carnegie Project on the Education Doctorate Convening, Pittsburgh, PA.

Kumar, S., & Dawson, K. (2018). *An online doctorate for researching professionals: Program design, implementation, and evaluation*. Athabasca University Press.

Lively, C. L., Blevins, B., Talbert, S., & Cooper, S. (2021). Building community in online professional practice doctoral programs. *Impacting Education: Journal on Transforming Professional Practice, 6*(3), 21–29. https://doi.org/10.5195/ie.2021.187

Lovitts, B. E. (2007). *Making the implicit explicit: Creating performance expectations for the dissertation*. Stylus.

Perry, J. A. (2013). Carnegie Project on the Education Doctorate: The education doctorate—a degree for our time. *Planning & Changing, 44*(3/4), 113–126.

Peterson, D. S. (2017). Preparing scholarly practitioners: Redesigning the EdD to reflect CPED principles. *Impacting Education: Journal on Transforming Professional Practice, 2*(1). https://doi.org/10.519 5/ie.2017.30

Piantanida, M., McMahon, P. L., & Llewellyn, M. (2018). *On being a scholar-practitioner: Practical wisdom in action*. Learning Moments Press.

Rogers, E. M. (2003). *Diffusion of innovations* (5th ed.). The Free Press.

Schuster, M. T. (2017). *The EdD and the scholarly practitioner: The CPED path*. https://doi.org/10.5195/ie.2017.34

Shelton, R. N., Werse, N. R., Davis, B. K., & Franz, N. E. (2023). Scaffolding the research process: Mitigating imposter syndrome before the dissertation. In C. Benedetti & A. Covarrubias (Eds.), *Teaching critical inquiry and applied research in Ed.D. programs moving beyond traditional methods*. Meyers Press.

Walker-Schmidt, W., Kaul, C., & Crocker Papadakis, L. (2022). Onboarding effects on engagement and retention in the IT sector. *Impacting Education: Journal on Transforming Professional Practice, 7*(4), 8–15. https://doi.org/10.5195/ie.2022.220

Werse, N. R. (2021). Practical and transferable: The quest to design online writing instruction for mentoring professional doctoral students. In L. Gray-Rosendale & S. Rosendale (Eds.), *Go online! Reconfiguring writing courses for the new, virtual world*. Peter Lang.

Werse, N. R., Cooper, S., Meehan, J. P., & Sanguras, L. (2023). Designing dissertation courses for the dissertation in practice: Both dissertation and practice. In C. Benedetti & A. Covarrubias (Eds.), *Teaching critical inquiry and applied research in Ed.D. programs moving beyond traditional methods*. Meyers Press.

Werse, N. R., Lively, C., & Crocker Papadakis, L. (2022). High impact writing support for online students writing a dissertation in practice. In Information Resources Management Association (Ed.), *Research anthology on doctoral student professional development* (pp. 499–514). IGI Global.

Yeung, R. P. (2022). Understanding the relationship between white teacher implicit bias and Black student academic disparities and high discipline rates. In A. T. Adams (Ed.), *Advances in Educational Marketing, Administration, and Leadership* (pp. 23–51). IGI Global. https://doi.org/10.4018/978-1-6684-3359-1.ch002

CHAPTER EIGHT

And the Winner is . . . All of Us (?)

W. KYLE INGLE AND
HARRIETTE THURBER RASMUSSEN

In this edited volume, all of the contributing authors are faculty members at a Program of the Year (POY) Award-winning CPED institution. We asked them to tell the stories of their award-winning programs, discussing their innovative features and the processes through which the faculty and other stakeholders developed their programs. Our hope is that sharing their stories may inform the work of faculty in other Ed.D. programs. By featuring award-winning programs recognized for innovative designs and effectiveness, this volume becomes a strategy to diffuse innovative Ed.D. design features and stimulate change in Ed.D. programs—within CPED and beyond. It also explores the institutional opportunities of applying for an award such as this: opportunities for institutional growth, institutional coherence, and change ownership.

In this final chapter, we begin by providing a synthesis of the innovative elements and design features of the award-winning programs and their motivations for engaging in program analysis and (re)design. We also explore where and how they sought ideas for their award-winning Ed.D. programs and the ways in which they borrowed and adapted innovations from elsewhere, thus becoming agents of diffusion themselves. We also explore the various communication channels used by the authors and potential adopters of their innovative practices, gauging the extent to which faculty members at other institutions wanted to learn more about the award-winning programs. We admonish our readers about the importance of engaging in reflection for improving programs continuously and adapting to ever-constant forces of change. Lastly, we conclude by encouraging faculty in CPED-influenced Ed.D. programs to take their reflections and consider applying for the POY Award when they are ready so to do.

Innovations and Motivations among Award-Winning Programs

Rogers (2003) characterizes the innovation process within an organization as consisting of two broad activities: (1) initiation, consisting of all of the information gathering, conceptualization, and planning for the adoption of an innovation, leading up to the decision to adopt, and (2) implementation, consisting of all of the events, actions, and decisions involved in putting the innovation into use. Across all of the award-winning programs featured in our edited book, every one of them began with a desire to address what they perceived as a problem (or problems) in need of redress within their Ed.D. program.

In the case of the University of Missouri, the program faculty sought a more practitioner-relevant alternative to the traditional five-chapter model commonly found in Ph.D. programs for their statewide cooperative Ed.D. program. The program faculty at Arizona State University sought to identify and develop an approach to research that met the needs of working education professionals engaged in solving problems of practice—and one that facilitated the timely success of the scholar-practitioners that joined their Ed.D. Arizona State University eventually developed the use of cycles of action research (CARs) and leader scholar communities (LSCs) during the dissertation phase as their two signature pedagogies featured in their award-winning application. The University of Hawaiʻi at Mānoa responded to concerns expressed by practicing educational leaders regarding the applicability and relevance of a Ph.D. to educational practice. These concerns and their search for solutions shaped the development of their Group Consultancy Project (GCP) and the Dissertation in Practice (DiP) in their Ed.D. in Professional Educational Practice. The faculty in Baylor University's Department of Curriculum and Education sought to increase enrollments and improve the quality of their Ed.D. in Learning and Organizational

Change. They expanded the concept of *educator* to fields beyond early childhood, K–12, and higher education, increasing the program's reach, enrollment, and diversity.

Other award-winning institutions sought to address structural and/or policy barriers within their program, college, or university in their efforts to improve the instruction of scholar-practitioners in their Ed.D. For example, Drexel University's Ed.D. in Leadership and Management sought improvements to mentoring and advising systems to meet the needs of a large number of students enrolled in the program. The faculty associated with the University of Florida's Ed.D. in Teachers, Schools, and Society pursued institutional policy changes to shift the content and focus of research courses in their program, all the while seeking to build and maintain the support and collegial relationships with faculty members responsible for instruction in research and evaluation methods.

Looking for Solutions—Borrowing and Adapting Innovative Ed.D. Practices

Researchers note that an innovation is a policy or practice perceived as new to the unit (e.g., US states, school districts, universities), adopting it regardless of its age, whether it exists elsewhere, or how many other units have adopted it (Cohen-Vogel & Ingle, 2007; Walker, 1969; Gray, 1973; Berry, 1994). Education policy scholars note two schools of thought on how and why a state policy innovation may diffuse across US states. One is regional diffusion, which holds that decision-makers at the state level simplify the task of finding policy solutions by borrowing ideas from neighboring states (Walker, 1969). Motivated by the pressures of interstate competition, formal and informal networks develop between regional policymakers, promoting and furthering the diffusion of an innovative policy (Dye, 1990; Cohen-Vogel et al., 2008). The other is that of internal determinants, such that the internal characteristics and conditions within a given unit (e.g., U.S. states) contribute to whether or not an innovation is adopted. In other words, the states that adopt an innovation do so when the political, economic, and social environments are favorable (Gray, 1973).

Take, for instance, research that has explored the diffusion of a specific higher education policy, broad-based merit aid scholarship programs in the United States. Researchers have examined the adoption and nonadoption of broad-based merit aid in the southeastern United States (Cohen-Vogel & Ingle, 2007; Ingle et al., 2007; Ness & Mistretta, 2010) and beyond (Ingle & Petroff, 2013). These researchers suggest that internal determinants facilitated or prevented the adoption of broad-based merit aid within their state contexts. One might wonder, *what is so innovative about a scholarship?* After all, financial support for students has long existed in the United States. Anne Radcliffe, Lady Mowlson of London, left a bequest to Harvard in 1643, providing financial support to students in need (Harvard College, n.d.). Scholarships were not a new phenomenon, but broad-based merit aid programs funded by the state, having no income cap, and eligibility requirements met by a substantial proportion of the adopting states' high school graduates were a new take on a pre-existing concept (Cohen-Vogel & Ingle, 2007). Although all state broad-based merit aid programs sought to reward K–12 academic performance with public scholarships for postsecondary education, the eligibility criteria and award amounts differed from state to state and program to program.

Similarly, the innovative program practices and policies featured in these chapters vary from one award-winning institution to the other. Whether looking for an alternative to the traditional five-chapter dissertation (University of Missouri), meeting the needs of expanded enrollments (Drexel), or improving curricular components of an Ed.D. program (University of Florida), the award-winning institutions featured in this edited volume explored their options, and adapted various innovative solutions and practices to address what they perceived as programmatic problems within their Ed.D. programs. Indeed, the closest thing to an overarching innovation that cuts across all the institutions is the extent to which they have successfully adopted and implemented the CPED Framework, its design concepts, and principles. The specifics of these (re)design efforts vary greatly from one award-winning institution to the next, thus honoring the local context of each member institution within the CPED consortium (CPED, n.d.). Indeed, all nominees for the CPED

POY award had to delineate their Ed.D. programs' alignment with the CPED framework, its design concepts, and principles as part of the application process if they were to remain in contention for the annual award. This component of the application process remains a part of the CPED POY Award to this day.

One can conceive the pressures of competition among institutions of higher learning. In the academic marketplace, there remains stiff competition for students and the edge over competitors in terms of program design and delivery (Dill, 2003; Wladis et al., 2023). As we mentioned in Chapter 1, winning the POY Award represents a valuable point of pride for the university and program as well as a valuable recruitment tool for the program. As to the other school of thought, the internal determinants of Ed.D. programs, such as the desire to differentiate between traditional Ph.D. and Ed.D. program, to improve mentoring and advising practices, or adapt research methods for students may serve as motivating factors for Ed.D. programs to (re)design, drawing upon CPED's network, resources, framework, and experience for inspiration.

Our contributing authors discussed their pursuit of possible alternatives as involving both internal and external sources for ideas and collaboration. Internally, faculty from these award-winning programs (e.g., Drexel, University of Missouri, University of Hawai'i at Mānoa) involved key stakeholders such as current students and alumni from their programs. Externally, the award-winning Ed.D. faculty members looked to extant research to inform their decision making. For example, faculty at the University of Missouri described establishing a task force that explored alternative formats of dissertations in practice that balanced rigor and fit for scholar-practitioners by reviewing and citing relevant research, such as Archbald (2008) and Olson and Clark (2009). Furthermore, the faculty at the University of Missouri discussed reviewing materials collected from CPED convenings, the CPED website, and program websites from other institutions of higher learning. The contributing authors from institutions such as Baylor, Drexel, and the University of Hawai'i at Mānoa discussed the importance of communicating and involving external stakeholders, such as educational and industry leaders to inform their programs' understanding of the problems and possible innovative solutions. The faculty members associated with the University of Florida's Ed.D. in Teachers, Schools, and Society sought to build support and collegiality among colleagues within the College of Education in their efforts to change college policies as well as the content and focus of research and evaluation courses in the Ed.D. program.

Diffusing Innovative Ed.D. Practices across the Consortium and Beyond

In creating and bestowing the POY Award, CPED seeks to recognize programs for their distinctive, innovative, and impactful designs and practices, but it also seeks to serve as a means of diffusing these program innovations across its membership and beyond. In other words, CPED, its member institutions, and faculty emerge as a social system that engages in developing and diffusing innovative features across Ed.D. programs. Our contributing authors discussed their role in diffusing these practices at annual convenings via the awards ceremony and invited learning exchanges. Furthermore, CPED highlights the award-winning programs for its membership and the public by means of the consortium's website. The contributing authors also noted their efforts to share information about their innovative programs and practices by means of CPED's *Impacting Education: The Journal for Transforming Professional Practice* (IE) or other existing peer-reviewed journals.

Then there are the personal contacts made in the wake of winning a CPED POY Award. These took place face-to-face at CPED annual convenings, online at CPED convenings (during the pandemic), and electronically via email contacts. Faculty members from award-winning institutions noted responding to such inquiries from those at other institutions seeking further details about the innovative programs and their potential compatibility within their own local contexts. These provide evidence of the importance of initial or early adopters as *proofing sites* (Imig et al., 2009) to other potential later adopters. Faculty members at award-winning institutions also reported receiving and responding to inquiries seeking helpful hints, advice for constructing application materials, and any competitive edge that they could glean from the correspondence. These may provide some evidence of an analog for interstate competition found in state policy diffusion.

After the Award Ceremony—The March of Time and Change

Contributing authors from award-winning programs reflected upon the impact of the award on their Ed.D. programs and how their programs have continued to adapt and innovate after winning. In spite of reporting benefits (e.g., increased enrollment, institutional recognition, external recognition, success in approving faculty lines), becoming an award-winning CPED program did not shelter them from the ever-present forces of change and time. The contributing authors reported engaging in continuous review and evaluation of their programs and their various components, whether admissions, coursework, comprehensive examinations, structures of dissertations in practice, etc. This is to be expected. After all, CPED is a consortium that encourages and facilitates its members critically examining their Ed.D. programs through dialog, experimentation, critical feedback, and evaluation.

In essence, the authors note that there is no time to rest on one's laurels. Continuous reflection, evaluation, and improvement are integral to graduate programs if they are to survive and thrive. In fact, we, the editors, might argue that innovations should never be static. The rapidly changing context for successful Ed.D. programs by itself seems to cement that assumption. This is especially so in the face of changing economic conditions and the academic marketplace. Fellabaum-Toston and colleagues (Chapter 2) from the University of Missouri discussed the challenges their award-winning statewide cooperative Ed.D. program faced due to financial deficits and changes in their institution's budget model. As a result, their Statewide Cooperative Ed.D. Program transitioned back to a single-institution program. In contrast, Buss and Marsh (Chapter 3) of Arizona State University reported their program faculty members engaging in slight modifications in response to accommodating enrollment growth and onboarding new faculty members. Likewise, program faculty from Drexel reported program tinkering in their efforts to continuously evaluate and improve their program, engaging in revisions to new student orientations, student assessments, course scaffolding, and sequencing. Contributing authors from one of the more recent award-winning programs (Baylor University) report exploring efforts for how they will sustain their award-winning program to ensure it continues to evolve, improve, and provide meaningful experiences for students, faculty, and alumni alike.

Program faculty in the University of Hawai'i's Ed.D. program in Professional Educational Practice reported their commitment to engaging with program stakeholders in continuous program improvement efforts in spite of numerous challenges they faced after winning the POY Award. These challenges included leadership changes at the program and college levels, the loss of some external funder support, budgetary issues, and stubborn concerns that remain regarding the academic rigor of the Ed.D. Interestingly, the University of Hawai'i at Mānoa reported a reduction in applications to its Ed.D. program after winning the award for 2018, suggesting that even external recognition has its limits in the face of local education markets and institutional conditions.

Program faculty at the University of Florida reported both internal and external policies and politics that affected their Ed.D. program after receiving the POY award. Internally, their Ed.D. program faculty have since attempted to change the Graduate School's policies regarding who can serve as dissertation chairs, on committees, and the processes by which one earns Graduate Faculty Status (GFS) at their institution. The institution's current policies continue to exclude doctoral-holding educational practitioners in the community from serving on committees as well as new faculty members not yet eligible for GFS. These constraints have hindered growth in their program in spite of winning the coveted POY Award, leading to inadequate numbers of faculty with GFS, decreased capacity with existing faculty members, and lost opportunities to capitalize on valuable perspectives and experiences of practicing education professionals holding doctorates.

The continued adaptation of these programs in response to multiple factors may, we argue, have been aided by routinized internal processes explained in these chapters—self-study, reflection, response to internal and external forces, stakeholder involvement—habits that were developed and/or enhanced through the application process itself.[1] In some cases, these have been sufficient to respond to external policies. For others, the changing policy and political landscape cautions against broader assertion and prediction. The contributing authors from the University of Florida note the challenges associated with legislation enacted by a Republican-dominated legislature. While not named specifically in their chapter, Adams et al. (Chapter 6) allude to Florida Senate Bill 266, which Republican Governor Ron DeSantis signed into law in May 2023. The legislation prohibits Florida public colleges and universities from spending funds on activities or programs that "advocate for diversity, equity, and inclusion, or promote or engage in political or social activism, as defined by rules of the State Board of Education and regulations of the Board of Governors." The legislation also seeks to protect what it calls "viewpoint diversity" on college campuses, in training related to civic education, open inquiry, and in civil discourse. The University of Florida's Ed.D. program was designed to align with the CPED framework, which includes committing to "questions of equity, ethics, and social justice to bring about solutions to complex problems of practice" (CPED, n.d., Guiding Principle #1). Given their Ed.D. program's equity focus and the pressure on K–12 practitioners (who the program serves) to avoid discussions of race, sexual orientation, and basic historical facts (e.g., impacts of slavery), the program faculty at the University of Florida find themselves grappling with the potential impacts of the legislation on their award-winning program. Their questions revolve around the social justice emphasis of their award-winning program and the impact of the legislation on the topics students pursue. Given these recent developments, it remains too early to tell if the University of Florida, a member of the prestigious Association of American Universities, will see a decrease in its rankings from influential producers of such metrics like *US News and World Report* (USNWR). The methodology for USNWR's rankings includes expert opinion from academicians selected to rate the academic quality of peer institutions with which they are familiar (US News & World Report, 2022). There are some early signs that

Florida's higher education policies and actions (e.g., changes in governance at New College) are having a chilling effect on the state of Florida's higher education institutions and faculty, contributing to an increase in faculty attrition and difficulties in staffing faculty and staff vacancies (Contreras, 2023). In sum, challenges remain in spite of external recognitions, such as the CPED POY Award.

In Closing

As noted in Chapter 1 of this edited book, we sought to shine a light on award-winning programs worthy of recognition and emulation. We wanted the authors from these institutions to tell their stories—how they designed their CPED-influenced Ed.D. programs, how they sought to innovate their programs, where they looked for guidance, best practices, structures, and processes, as well as how they determined the effectiveness of their programs and the impacts on their graduates and communities. The heart of this book is the process stories of these award-winning institutions as they sought to further institutional and programmatic goals through innovation and impact. We hope that it is indeed more than just *show-and-tell.* The faculty involved in the design and delivery of the award-winning programs took the time and effort required to apply for these awards, and in so doing, they incurred opportunity costs—the costs incurred when allocating resources (e.g., one's time) for one particular purpose and not for another (Levin & McEwan 2001). Having won CPED's POY Award, one may conclude in hindsight that their investment of time and energy in applying paid off. However, this was an unknown at that time. They did so without any assurance that their efforts would be rewarded with the desired outcome—being selected as the award winner.

Should the readers of this book be faculty members at a CPED member institution and associated with an Ed.D. program, we hope that the potential for high opportunity costs will not deter them from applying for the CPED POY award. We contend that even if a nominated Ed.D. program is not selected as an award winner, the program, its faculty, and students can benefit from the process of self-study that is part and parcel of the application process.

We leave the readers who may want to consider applying for the CPED POY Award, or other types of institutional awards, with some advice from the Program of the Year Award's current co-chairs and some of the faculty from award-winning programs. First, we offer advice as co-chairs. Look for the opportunities in the process itself, as while you may benefit from winning the award, that is never a given, but the opportunity cost of applying for this award is, we argue, realized through the lasting benefits of self-study, critical reflection, and authentic engagement—ownership—of choices made in programmatic design. And, importantly, consider how you will recognize the impacts you seek from programmatic innovation and make those data a core part of your design. Concrete evidence related to successful innovations requires more than "we did it." No institution—or award-bestowing committee—should be satisfied with evidence of implementation only. Did it accomplish what was intended? Show us!

As to some advice from faculty at an institution that was successful in their submission, we point to Western Carolina University. While they were not able to submit a chapter for this edited book, they presented at a Pre-Convening Workshop titled, "How the Program of the Year (POY) Was Won: Will Your Program be the Next CPED Program of the Year?" (Rasmussen et al., 2021). Dr. Jess Weiler, associate professor of educational leadership, recommended a number of helpful hints from her and her fellow faculty members, the first of which is to give the application process plenty of time. Preparing an application for the award is not a process that lends itself to one intense writing session. It takes time to reflect on one's program and generate an application. Second, Dr. Weiler and colleagues recommended integrating the entire program faculty in the application process. This should be a team effort, not just a program coordinator or select single faculty member doing it all. Third, Dr. Weiler noted that, "there are not enough pages for fluff." Fourth, use the rubrics to guide the development of your application—revisit from time to time and get multiple perspectives on the application requirements and criteria. Finally, Dr. Weiler and her colleagues recommended that the submitting faculty members share their program's authentic journey. With multiple years of chairing this committee, we can second this point. Some of the most powerful applications have been those that showed the growth and improvements made in a program because of their reflections and analyses. As noted above, these are the institutional impacts that outlive the glory of award recognition and the particular innovation that was recognized.

Will all of the featured POY Award-winning programs and their innovative features be emulated across all (or even some) of CPED's Ed.D. programs? Not necessarily. Doing so depends on a number of factors identified by Rogers (2003) and innovation diffusion scholars that have applied his theoretical framework in a broad range of fields of study, such as agriculture (e.g., Abdulai & Huffman, 2005), communications (e.g., Srivastava & Moreland, 2012), business (Brouthers et al., 2016), and health care (e.g., Berwick, 2003). Elementally, the diffusion of an innovation depends on four main elements. These include the nature of the innovation itself, the depths of the communications channels by which potential adopters may learn about the innovation, the time it takes between first learning about an innovation to adopting it, and how fast individuals, programs, and organizations adopt an innovation in a given period. This edited book adds to the potential means by which possible adopters may learn about innovative programs, features, and practices and, in turn, find benefit to their programs through innovation and diffusion.

Endnote

1. It could be assumed that the many unsuccessful POY winners also benefitted from the internal self-study processes explained by the authors in this volume.

References

Abdulai, A., & Huffman, W. E. (2005). The diffusion of new agricultural technologies: The case of crossbred-cow technology in Tanzania. *American Journal of Agricultural Economic, 87*(3), 537–821. https://doi.org/10.1111/j.1467-8276.2005.00753.x

Archbald, D. (2008). Research versus problem solving for the education leadership doctoral thesis: Implications for form and function. *Educational Administration Quarterly, 44*(5), 704–739. https://doi.org/10.1177/0013161X07313288

Berry, F. B. (1994). Sizing up state policy innovation research. *Policy Studies Journal, 22*(3), 442–456. https://doi.org/10.1111/j.1541-0072.1994.tb01480.x

Berwick, D. M. (2003). Disseminating innovations in health care. *Journal of the American Medical Association, 289*(15), 1969–1975. doi:10.1001/jama.289.15.1969

Brouthers, K. D., Geisser, K. D., & Rothlauf, F. (2016). Explaining the internationalization of ibusiness firms. *Journal of International Business Studies, 47*(5), 513–534. https://doi.org/10.1057/jibs.2015.20

Carnegie Project on the Education Doctorate (CPED). (n.d.). The CPED Framework. Retrieved August 28, 2023 from https://cped.memberclicks.net/the-framework

Cohen-Vogel, L., & Ingle, W. K. (2007). When neighbours matter most: Innovation, diffusion and state policy adoption in tertiary education. *Journal of Education Policy, 22*(3), 241–262. https://doi.org/10.1080/02680930701269152

Cohen-Vogel, L., Ingle, W. K., Levine, A. A., & Spence, M. (2008). The "spread" of merit-based college aid: Politics, policy consortia, and interstate competition. *Educational Policy, 22*(3), 339–362. https://doi.org/10.1177/0895904807307059

Contreras, J. (2023, July 30). "I'm not wanted": Florida universities hit by brain drain as academics flee. *The Guardian*. https://www.theguardian.com/us-news/2023/jul/30/florida-universities-colleges-faculty-leaving-desantis

Dill, D. D. (2003). Allowing the market to rule: The case of the United States. *Higher Education Quarterly, 57*(2), 136–157. https://doi.org/10.1111/1468-2273.00239

Dye, T. R. (1990). *American federalism: Competition among governments*. Lexington Books.

Gray, V. (1973). Innovations in the states: a diffusion study. *American Political Science Review, 67*, 1174–1191. https://www.jstor.org/stable/1956539

Harvard College. (n.d.). History of financial aid. Retrieved August 29, 2023 from https://college.harvard.edu/about/mission-vision-history/history-financial-aid

Imig, D., Perry, J. A., & Syed, S. (2009). *Creating rubrics for the assessment of the Ed.D.: Narrative report to the Spencer Foundation*. Carnegie Project on the Education Doctorate.

Ingle, W. K., Cohen-Vogel, L., & Hughes, R. (2007). The public policy process among southeastern states: Elaborating theories of regional adoption and holdout behavior. *Policy Studies Journal, 35*(4), 607–628. https://doi.org/10.1111/j.1541-0072.2007.00239.x

Ingle, W. K., & Petroff*, R. A. (2013) Public entrepreneurs and the adoption of broad-based merit aid beyond the Southeastern United States. *Education Policy Analysis Archives, 21*(58), 1–28. http:/epaa.asu.edu/ojs/article/view/1252

Levin, H. M., & McEwan, P. J. (2001). *Cost-effectiveness analysis, 2nd edition*. Sage.

Ness, E. C., & Mistretta, M. (2010). Merit aid in North Carolina: A case study of a "non-event." *Educational Policy, 24*(5), 703–734. https://doi.org/10.1177/0895904809339165

Olson, K., & Clark, C. M. (2009). A signature pedagogy in doctoral education: The leader-scholar community. *Educational Researcher, 38*(3), 216–221. https://doi.org/10.3102/0013189X09334207

Rasmussen, H. T., Ingle, W. K., Hill, D., Jeter, G., & Weiler, J. (2021, October 19). How the Program of the Year (POY) was won: Will your program be the next CPED Program of the Year? A Pre-Convening Workshop held at the Virtual Convening of the Carnegie Project on the Education Doctorate.

Rogers, E. M. (2003). *Diffusions of innovations* (5th ed.). The Free Press.

Srivastava, J., & Moreland, J. J. (2012) Diffusion of innovations: Communication evolution and influences. *Communication Review, 15*(4), 294–312. http://dx.doi.org/10.1080/10714421.2012.728420

US News and World Report. (2022). How U.S. News calculated the 2022–2023 Best Colleges Rankings. https://www.usnews.com/education/best-colleges/articles/how-us-news-calculated-the-rankings

Walker, J. L. (1969). The diffusion of innovations among the American states. *American Political Science Review, 63*(3), 880–899. https://www.jstor.org/stable/1954434

Wladis, C., Hachey, A. C., & Conway, A. (2023). Time poverty: A hidden factor connecting online enrollment and college outcomes. *Journal of Higher Education, 94*(5), 609–637. https://doi.org/10.1080/00221546.2022.2138385

ABOUT THE AUTHORS

Alyson Adams is a Clinical Professor in the Teachers, Schools, & Society program, and Director for the School of Teaching & Learning at University of Florida. Her teaching and research focus largely around online graduate programs for practicing educators at the masters and doctorate levels in the areas of teacher leadership and professional learning.

Ray R. Buss is Professor of Educational Psychology and Educational Research in the Mary Lou Fulton Teachers College at Arizona State University. He conducts research on doctoral students' development of identities as educational leaders and educational researchers, examines other aspects of our Ed.D. program, and collaborates with colleagues on investigating technology integration by students in teacher preparation programs.

Sandi Cooper is Professor of Mathematics Education, Associate Chair of Curriculum and Instruction, and Coordinator of Mathematics Education. She is the Founding Director of the Online Ed.D. in Learning and Organizational Change in the School of Education at Baylor University. Dr. Cooper's research is focused on early number development, integrating children's literature into mathematics instruction, teacher noticing, and mathematical experiences in museums.

Bradley R. Curs is Associate Professor in the Department of Educational Leadership and Policy Analysis at the University of Missouri. His research uses tools from the discipline of economics to understand the effects of educational policy on higher education students and institutions.

Nancy Fichtman Dana is currently Professor of Education and Distinguished Teaching Scholar at the University of Florida. Her research focuses on professional learning, with a particular focus on practitioner research. She has published 12 books and over 100 articles and book chapters related to teachers', administrators', doctoral students', teacher candidates', and teacher educators' professional learning through inquiry.

Jennifer Fellabaum-Toston is the Senior Associate Dean for Student Success and Academic Affairs in the College of Education and Human Development at the University of Missouri. She is also an Associate Teaching Professor of Higher Education in the Department of Educational Leadership and Policy Analysis. Her research and teaching interests include identities in higher education, postsecondary teaching and learning, and the development of scholarly practitioners/practitioner-scholars.

Casandra Harper is Associate Professor of Higher Education in the Department of Educational Leadership and Policy Analysis at the University of Missouri, Columbia. She is also a Faculty Affiliate in the Department of Women's and Gender Studies. She studies the differential effect of college on students across a range of topics including: parent and family engagement in first-generation college students' lives, racial identity, student success, and how students and families navigate the financial aid process.

Deanna Hill is an Associate Clinical Professor and Program Director in the School of Education's Educational Leadership and Management Program and Higher Education Program. Dr. Hill's research interests include education law and policy, intersectionality, Critical Race Theory, educator workforce issues, and school choice.

Lori Ideta currently serves as the Vice Provost for Student Success at the University of Hawai'i at Mānoa. Dr. Ideta is also a tenured Faculty Specialist and graduate faculty member of the University of Hawai'i College of Education where she has served as the co-director of the Ed.D. in Professional Educational Practice Program.

W. Kyle Ingle is Professor of P–12 Educational Leadership in the Department of Educational Leadership, Evaluation, and Organizational Development at the University of Louisville. His research interests include human resource functions in education, the politics of education, and economic evaluations of education programs.

Gage Jeter previously coordinated the Ed.D. program in Teachers, Schools, and Society while working as a Clinical Assistant Professor in the School of Teaching and Learning at the University of Florida from 2018 to 2023. Now an Assistant Professor of English in the department of Language, Culture, and Gender Studies at Texas Woman's University, he supports preservice secondary English language arts teachers through teaching, research, and service centered on humanizing, process-oriented, and critical literacies in and beyond educational spaces.

Walter Kahumoku, III is the Executive Assistant to the Chancellor at the University of Hawai'i West O'ahu and the former Director of the Kauhale Kīpaipai (Educator Professional Development) Department of the Kamehameha Schools. Dr. Kahumoku has dedicated his life's work to improving the educational wellbeing of Hawai'ian learners as a former high school teacher, writing specialist, school administrator, and faculty member. He provides instruction in teacher and administrator education, curriculum development, instructional strategies, assessment, professional development, and educational policy.

Josephine P. Marsh is Associate Professor of Literacy Education in the Mary Lou Fulton Teachers College at Arizona State University (ASU) and chair of the Leadership and Innovation Ed.D. program. Her research focuses on literacy professional development and peer coaching, sustaining literacy communities of practice for professional growth, adolescent literacy engagement and learning, and the impact of practitioner research in and on local educational settings.

Elizabeth Anne Murray is a Graduate Writing Coordinator in the Research and Writing Development Center at Baylor University for the Ed.D. program in Learning and Organizational Change. She also serves as an Affiliate Clinical Professor in the School of Education at Baylor University. Her research interests include disruptive encounters with literature, difficult conversations in English Language Arts classrooms, and the intersections of literature, learning, and morality.

Lacy Crocker Papadakis is Assistant Director of the Research and Writing Development Center in the Ed.D. in Learning and Organizational Change program and an Affiliate Clinical Professor in the School of Education at Baylor University.

Jill A. Perry is Professor of Practice in the School of Education at the University of Pittsburgh. Her research focuses on professional doctorate preparation in education, organizational change in higher education, and faculty leadership roles. She also serves as the Executive Director of the Carnegie Project on the Education Doctorate (CPED), a consortium of more than 130 colleges and schools of education dedicated to transforming the advanced preparation of educational professionals to lead through scholarly practice for the improvement of individuals and communities.

Harriette Thurber Rasmussen is an Assistant Clinical Professor in the Ed.D. program in Educational Leadership and Management at Drexel University. Her research focuses on online teaching and learning, adult development, organizations, adaptive capacity, organizational effectiveness, teacher efficacy, and accountability in education systems.

Laila Sanguras is a Lecturer in the Department of Curriculum & Instruction and graduate program director of the Ed.D. in Learning and Organizational Change. Dr. Sanguras' areas of teaching include educational evaluation and mixed methods research. Her research focuses on the development of psychosocial skills as well as teacher and parent supports that facilitate student success.

Nicholas R. Werse is the Director for the Ed.D. Research and Writing Development Center in the Baylor University Ed.D. in Learning and Organizational Change Program and Affiliate Clinical Faculty in the Department of Curriculum and Instruction. When not mentoring doctoral writers, he pursues his research foci in the fields of religious studies, environmental humanities, and postgraduate education.

INDEX

D

E